MW00948213

I'm (No Longer) A Mormon

by

Regina Samuelson

ISBN-13: 978-1483940786

ISBN-10: 1483940780

Printed in the U.S.A.

First edition, November 2012

To all those who have struggled as I have,
Who have yet to struggle as I have,
And to those who love us anyway.

Introduction

Confessionals are all the rage lately, aren't they? And we don't have to wonder why: we all have this natural curiosity about the twisted lives of others.

I never thought of my life as twisted, never thought of my upbringing as odd, my college experience as sick, or the way I've tried to live my life as extremely screwed up…and yet, I'm guessing this book will demonstrate exactly how screwed up it has been.

I was raised Mormon, you see. I was raised by fabulous convert parents who did their darnedest (yup, "darnedest") to give their family a happy home. And they succeeded, for the most part. My childhood with my family was great.

But eventually you step back and look at all of the crazy crap that has gone on in your life through someone else's eyes, and you start to wonder how you ever made it through.

This is my story: the story of a Mormon girl who, well into her 30's, realized that she didn't believe in the Mormon faith. The story of what it's like for a really messed up lady to come to grips with the degree to which she is messed up, and what it's like to face her past, present, and future, wondering where to go from here.

A sibling asked why I'm bothering, why I need to "tell the world just how nuts the Mormon Church makes you." After all, most everyone I know is Mormon and happily living their life that way.

But *this is not for the Mormons I know.* I have no desire to disprove anyone's faith, to make them feel judged, duped, or stupid. We all have a path; if your path is Mormonism, I would never want to throw a stumbling block in your way. (Most of the time. Every once in a while I get a little rabid and wonder why no one else sees what I see, but I get over it.)

I'm concerned for people like myself: people with doubts, people who are contemplating leaving the LDS church – people who are leaving ANY faith where they've been thoroughly indoctrinated! – and people who have already left. It's a big scary world out there, and so many of us are unprepared and ill-equipped to deal with it. We need understanding and support from the world of which we were taught not to be a part.

"Normal" people don't know much about what it's like to be a Mormon. Even with Mitt Romney in the public eye, so few people have any idea of what it is Mormons believe…or what it's like to walk away from those beliefs.

It's you "normal" folk I'm hoping to reach. I need you to know what it's like inside my head (disturbing though that may sometimes be), so that when an indoctrinated friend of yours experiences a crisis of faith, you understand where they're coming from.

First, my disclaimers.

You will find a few four-letter words in this book. You will also discover that I waffle, that I have many great reasons to be horribly embarrassed by my past behaviors, and that I have absolutely no idea what I believe these days…hence some of my waffling. All my beliefs are subject to change. If ever I "come out" about my having written this book (no, my name is not Regina), I may very well believe something entirely differently than I do right now. I'm still figuring things out. Please be patient. If I say something offensive, something with which you do not agree, or something totally foolhardy, it's meant neither to offend, nor to challenge. I'm just trying to sort through a head full of brainwashing and discards…namely, Mormonism.

I feel no bitterness toward the LDS *people*, and though I've encountered a gossip or two in my day, I assure you there is no giant chip on my shoulder. I have nothing against "the saints". I have felt, however, and continue to experience, resentment toward the LDS faith toward the agony of the adjustment required to feel normal. If I'm ticked at Brigham, there's good reason, but it doesn't mean I'm ticked at my Mormon neighbor for being Mormon, nor does it mean that I blame Mormons in general for my difficulty in adjusting to the "real" world (or for their refusal, conscious or not, to accept it).

Beware information overload, ranging from historical tidbits to modern day miseries, incidents, and tales of major red flags in my life. I will do my best to cite what I can, but for in-depth studies into LDS history, I'd suggest reading Fawn Brodie, Ann Eliza Webb, John D. Lee, Bill Hickman, or Fanny Stenhouse. For modern-day issues, read Kay Burningham, Lyndon Lamborn, Park Romney, Martha Beck, or Lee Baker.

With regard to stories from my own life (and those from the lives of others, some of which are hearsay), I assure you they are true to the best of my knowledge and remembrance. I'm only passing on what I have heard from those close to me or experienced myself. (Most every name in this book has been changed, of course, including my own, both to protect the innocent *and* the guilty.) My memory may indeed be flawed, but consider, if you will, that the way I remember some of my own experiences is colored by my Mormon upbringing, and so if my perception of any of those experiences is "off" or peculiar, it is likely due to the psychological damage I have sustained as a Mormon. (The point is how what I remember, flawed or not, shaped my psyche.)

In other words, if at any point I sound crazy, well, I'm being up front about my craziness…and it's likely that it was Mormonism that made me nuts. I'm still trying to sort it all out. Please take what I say with a grain of salt and try to see whatever it is you're baffled by through my LDS-colored lenses (read: fogged up). I'm offering you a look into the warped brain of the brainwashed, and it's not always comfortable in here. My apologies, but thank you in advance for your patient understanding.

To give you an idea of this book's layout, the first section introduces me, Mormonism, and my broadest experience in it. The second section covers what it's *really* like to be a Mormon, including some of the thought patterns and expectations inherent in the beliefs. Section three discusses the issues (read: lies) in historical Mormonism that have most affected my life and psyche, and four discusses those same issues in the modern church. The fifth section is the juicy stuff (so if you're reading this for the "confessional" section, skip right to it!): a review of some of the incidents and red flags in my own life and those of my peers that caused me to question my faith. Some are funny, some are sick, and some are utterly baffling; brace yourself if you're sensitive. The sixth and final section of this book asks the question, "Now what?"

Not everyone is going to agree with what I have to offer here, nor will every – or even any – Mormon have had a similar experience. Not everyone will like it, believe it, or even bother to wade through it all. That's just fine; I'm not expecting to make friends with this book. The bottom line is that my massive, debilitating, life-long guilt has evolved into desperation for understanding, both for myself and others in my position, and I'm risking A HELL OF A LOT by opening my mouth.

But thank you for reading. Thank you for wanting to understand and support me through my personal journey, and more especially, for wanting to understand the experience of all of us leaving any faith. For those of us walking away from decades of indoctrination, *we need your support.*

How badly? Well, since this *is* a confessional, I'd like to share with you an entry in my journal from a few years back:

"Some Sundays I just can't bloody do it.

"Odd, really, because it all SEEMS to be going just fine: everyone's bathed, dressed, primped, and ready, including me, we actually get to church on time, and everyone gets off to their nursery/primary/RS meetings [toddler, children, and adult female "Relief Society" meetings] sans tears. (I include myself in the sans-tears bit as an accomplishment when attending our ward's RS, sadly.) Things are sane and normal during church, and perhaps I even have someone to sit by during RS. The lesson I taught goes just fine, even though I didn't have more than 5 minutes to plan it. I pick up my kids from their classes and they've had a great time, and we sit in sacrament with a few other young couples willing to help with the kids. And though [my first child] still can't talk in a whisper to save his life, and [my second child] wants desperately to get down and wander, that's really nothing unusual.

"But when my [child] asks to use the potty shortly after the sacrament is passed, it's all I can do to collect my things and my kids, drag them both to the bathroom, guard the door to the toilet, and then load them up in the car to head home.

"Seriously, is it hormones? Random depression surges? Emotional instability? Lack of a decent testimony? Pent up resentment of my husband's calling? An unconscious loathing of motherhood, for Heaven's sake?! I don't know! I just couldn't bring myself to sit in that chapel for even one more stinking minute! I felt like I was going to get up and scream and start throwing things...like I was going to leave my kids on a pew and vanish into the night...like I was going to go totally ape – $#*% and run up to the stand screaming livid judgments into the microphone until they dragged me off and had me committed.

"Why the extremes?! I'm a normal, generally rational person, and of course I prevented myself from doing any of the above, came home, changed into regular clothes with the kids and then baked some bread...but even now as I write this, I have this crazy inner turmoil bubbling in my chest. Am I just due for my period? Is it that limbo is suddenly catching up to me: 2 kids, can't have more, declined my dream job in favor of staying home some MORE as a "single parent" with a husband who works crap hours and then churches crap hours, no savings, no time or opportunity to pursue interests, and just generally tearing my hair out? We have no routine, no normalcy, and I feel like a failure at the one job I DO have because I resent my circumstances so badly.

"I'm gonna pop. WHAT THE HELL?

"There's the flipside, of course: fabulous husband, adorable kids, the ability I have to stay home with them, and time to bake bread…right? So why not look at the positives? Because right now I'm wallowing in my discomfort, in my consternation, in my desperation, thank you very much. And if I'd had to sit in church (I didn't; I left!) through two talks from missionaries about how I'm not doing enough to bring people to the truth and be harped on to take on *more* Godly responsibility, I swear I'd have just broken down and cried in sacrament. Not from the spiritual experience, but from an encroaching nervous breakdown.

"I just want to get on with crap, you know? Get out of this Godforsaken state, rip my husband away from the bishopric, say "screw you" to his job, create college funds for my kids, and go on a goddamn honeymoon. Oh, and take a vacation from church for a month or two. And not call anyone for those same couple months until I've worked all the grumpy ungodliness out of me and have had some semblance of sanity returned to my currently festering brain with all my friends and acquaintances knowing not to worry, I'll be in touch when I'm a decent person again.

"Instead of, you know, the girl who sat through RS today trying alternately not to fall asleep or raise her hand and tell off all the ladies in the room. The girl who dropped off her child at nursery, and when that child started to cry, turned her back, walked out, and pulled the door closed. The girl who bs'd her way through a lesson because she didn't know who had her book and furthermore just didn't care. The girl who took the sacrament because it was in front of her instead of focusing on the point and repenting silently of all her fallacies from the past week. The girl who left church an hour early so as to avoid unjustly and cruelly berating everyone who came within 3 feet of her. The girl who wonders every week when the hell her husband will be home from church thanks to his stupid calling so he can make dinner for a change and she can selfishly cast her kids from the kitchen while she whips up a new recipe for corn pudding she's been wanting to try out. The woman currently ignoring her own blood playing in the next room while she writes in her MORMON FUCKING JOURNAL. *That* girl.

"'Cause she's kind of a selfish, crazy, overly-emotive bitch on the verge of a random inexplicable breakdown. What IS wrong with me? Mormonism?"

Yup, folks, I actually said it. (Not the "F"-word part, but yes, I did actually say that, too.) 5 years ago – I hadn't even considered the possibility that I might not believe in the church at that point! – and already I knew that it was Mormonism that had thrown me for a loop…my entire life long.

This is why I write to you now. I – *we* – NEED YOU.

Section 1:
I'm (no longer) a Mormon

You've seen the ads: "I'm a Mormon." Most of them feature some fantastically successful ethnic person you never imagined could fit the stereotype. What stereotype is that? You know, the Mormon Mental Picture: a nuclear family with two blonde, blue-eyed parents, four kids, all blonde (two boys, two girls, of course), standing outside their Utah suburban home with a golden retriever sitting on the well-manicured lawn behind them. If you associate Mormons more easily with the FLDS sects – 10 wives, no make-up, homemade dresses, big bouffant braids – you're still baffled by the "I'm a Mormon" ads because it's *still* not what you were expecting. And that's what those Mormon ads want you to do: scratch your head and think, "Wow, I never knew they had Asian Mormons!" or "Check that out! That woman is a Mormon from India!" You're supposed to be amazed. Awed. Inspired.

I could put up my own ad: "I'm No Longer a Mormon." (Note: a friend told me just yesterday that there are "I'm an Ex-Mormon" ads up already. I'm a little late, I guess.) Anyway, I could post such an ad, and I don't know how well it would go over, but I imagine it might get a few chuckles.

That's not enough.

30-some years in lifelong cult-like agony is worth more than a few chuckles.

I'd at least appreciate a guffaw.

The title page of the Book of Mormon explains that it is written "to the convincing of the Jew and Gentile that Jesus is the Christ…" This book is a confessional-style tell-all to the convincing of the Jew and Gentile that the Mormonism I've experienced is a holy terror.

How so?

Mormonism – to an outsider – is INCOMPREHENSIVELY ALL-ENCOMPASSING. Every aspect of your life, every association you have, everything you do, every conversation in which you engage, EVERY SINGLE THING about your life has something to do with being a Mormon. When you wake in the morning, you're supposed to roll out of bed and onto your knees to start the day with prayer. You're supposed to read your scriptures for at least half an hour – preferably the Book of Mormon – either in the morning or evening, or really whenever you get the chance. (A friend of mine wandered into an LDS seminary room once and saw a sign on the wall that blew him away: "Before your homework, READ YOUR SCRIPTURES!" No joke.) After morning prayers come family prayers; some families say a family prayer before bed at night, some first thing in the morning, some both. Then there's breakfast, and you pray before eating…usually something to do with "nourishing and strengthening" your body. (It's a Mormon prayer catch-phrase lifted from the scriptures.) If you're in high school outside of Arizona or Utah (Mormon "Mecca"), you have early-morning seminary, which means basically an hour-long 6 AM Bible study class. You pray your way throughout the day, you smile warmly at non-members (because who knows but a simple comment from you could plant the seed of conversion in their hearts!), you chat on and off with your social network – mostly Mormon – all day long, pray silently at lunch, out loud with your family over dinner (since you're having dinner at home, like a good LDS family), and if it's Monday night, you have family night: a gospel lesson, a hymn, a couple prayers, and an activity. Don't forget to pray before bed, too! (And be sure not to let your prayers get repetitive; God doesn't like that.) If it's a Sunday, add 3 hours of church, no television or music (except Mormon stuff), and a crock pot dinner.

No, not all Mormons live like that, but it IS the gold standard…a veritable righteousness competition! And then we add on things like writing in your journal daily (*be sure to include only uplifting and spiritual things for the sake of your children's heritage!* It would reflect poorly on the church if you passed down that you were SAD as a Mormon!), attending any and all church meetings during the week in relation to your calling – your unpaid church assignment "from God" – and for heaven's sake, SMILE. We're a blessed and happy people, after all!

I was born into this. My parents converted to Mormonism together just prior to starting their family, but since they were married in the temple before my siblings and I came along, we were "Born in the Church." My entire family got a really big kick out of abbreviating that when we were kids: We are a bunch of B.I.T.CH-es. What should that tell you about my family? That my siblings and I were raised by heretics and hedonists, God bless them. My parents, in other words, are more normal than most LDS parents, having attained adulthood without the influence of the LDS faith affecting their childhoods. They were nowhere near as strict, and always more flexible than the parents of my LDS peers. (The idea that we used the word "bitch" in our home – particularly in reference to something church-related! – still horrifies some of my LDS friends.)

Though we were more flexible than most, what we did take seriously, as does every other member of the LDS church, were accusations that we were not Christian. We could laugh at ourselves, but could not stand the idea that others were laughing at us. (This is a pretty strong theme in the church.) To this day, the very best way to enrage a Mormon is to tell them that they are "not really Christian."

If you're a Christian, you've probably decided long ago that Mormons aren't Christian. After all, we don't believe Jesus is God, we don't believe in the trinity, and we have Christ showing up some time after his death in the Americas. Doesn't sound like any Jesus you know, does it? But you will NEVER, EVER win a Mormon friend with this point of view, nor will you ever understand where they're coming from.

You've probably noticed by now that sometimes I include myself with the Mormons and sometimes I don't. Bear with me. I still struggle.

Mormons KNOW themselves to be Christian. They believe that not only do they know and love Jesus Christ as a savior the same way that the rest of the Christian populace does, they know Him *even better*! They know that He spent time in the Americas. They know that He restored His original church through Joseph Smith, unmolested by centuries of apostasy. They believe He is the head of the church and the Redeemer of all. In fact, based on the general Christian belief in the trinity, they think they know the REAL Christ better than mainstream Christianity. It's not meant as an insult to Christians, it's a conviction that they TRULY love Jesus Christ, and they are horribly insulted and offended when anyone suggests that they've got it wrong and aren't Christian.

I admit, Mormons do seem to have some really insane beliefs…primarily when taken out of context. I won't bother to launch into them here – most you can study on your own at Mormon.org, the church's website – but suffice it to say that when your whole life is built around the framework and explanation of the LDS church, believing the Garden of Eden was in Missouri isn't much of a stretch. By the time you hit adulthood, you know all about it; you've covered all sorts of peculiar "facts" in gospel doctrine classes for years, and probably have heard more about the temple, tithing, prayer, fasting, and service than you've ever heard Jesus's name mentioned in class. (There is so much to LDS doctrine, I couldn't ever cover it all. Volume upon volume has been written about it, and so I won't try. The point is, by the time you've covered all the other "important" details in gospel doctrine or seminary on any given day, you probably haven't had much opportunity to actually say anything about Jesus…)

Exactly how long does it take to learn all this, to absorb all the details and doctrines, to make certain the Plan of Salvation is fully engrained? A lifetime, to be sure, but you're taught during childhood, during your youth, during 4 years of early-morning (or in UT and AZ, release-time) seminary, AND 4 years at BYU if you attend a churchi-versity…then you go on a mission and/or marry in the temple, receive a calling that requires you to study, learn, and cultivate your faith, and "endure to the end," meaning you keep moving forward…*in the church.*

Some of these things are optional. Seminary is optional…though you'll horrify your peers if you're a teen and don't attend, and be stared down by other members if you're not sending your children to seminary. Other things are NOT optional: for boys, you'd *better* serve a mission. (We love to make it *seem* optional, but it's *not*.) If you're a girl, you *must* marry a returned missionary in the temple. Not just any guy in the temple; a RETURNED MISSIONARY. And not just a returned missionary; it must be IN THE TEMPLE. Anything less is potential self-damnation. As a girl, you are raised *knowing* you'll marry a returned missionary in the temple…as soon as possible. You're desperate for it. So desperate, in fact, that it consumes your thoughts constantly.

Case-in-point, and my first embarrassing story: My freshman year at BYU (because I, too, went there, hoping to get a bachelor's *and* an MRS. degree), a friend from the dorms got married. *Yes, she was 18, and no, she was not the only girl on my floor that got married during freshman year.* We dorm-mates attended the reception, and eventually she got around to throwing her bouquet. I'll be damned if I didn't scramble for that thing like it was solid gold. I pushed, shoved, and dove for that blasted bouquet, finally catching it…and falling flat on my rear.

And I celebrated.

(If only you could feel the cringe in my typing just now.)

I cringe at a lot of things I've done. (There are a few doozies coming up later in this book.) One of the things I cringe at is a statement I made to some roommates at the Y (the nickname of church-owned Brigham Young University in Provo, Utah) after a particularly terrible "I'm a sinner going to hell and there's no hope for me" meltdown. (Yes, I've had many of those.) You see, in the church, we have what we call Peter Priesthoods and Molly Mormons...the basic stereotype of a Mormon man or woman. I remember, after sobbing for a solid half-hour over my own worthlessness and sinfulness, stating "I could do it." What? asked my roommates. "I could be a Molly Mormon." What exactly does that include, you ask? I remember spelling it out to them, and having them agree that, *yes!*, I *could* be a Molly Mormon! A Mormon girl who got up early, went to bed at a reasonable hour, who tried to find the positive in life to put in her journal, who wore floral print dresses and didn't wear too much make-up and never watched an R-rated movie or drank caffeine. Okay, I confess, the floral print dress bit was a joke...but so supportive were my roommates of my desire to "change" and be more "Christ-like" and devote myself to being the kind of Mormon of which I could be proud, that the very next day I came home from my classes to a brand new floral-print "ugly Mormon" dress. I think it even had a square lace-edged collar in front; somewhere between FLDS and Amish.

And I failed. I couldn't be a Molly Mormon. I liked boys. Surprising, I know, considering I married one, but I also liked making out with boys. Which was all I did. 'Til I got to BYU. (Read: BYU corrupted me.) I couldn't be a Molly Mormon because I could no longer be a virginal bride. I was a *failure*.

There are certain expectations of a Mormon bride...and a Mormon husband too, though I don't think they get quite the stick end that we do. Mormon women are expected to work, believe it or not. They work (usually to put their husbands through school) until they begin having babies, and then all thought of career goes out the window in order to become a stay-at-home Mom. I remember very clearly the day it occurred to me – it was a month before our wedding date – that my teaching career wouldn't last forever. I had wanted to be a teacher since childhood, had graduated in teaching, and was about to be married and start that teaching career. My fiancé and I were chatting about how soon into marriage we'd start a family, and when we came upon "two or three years" it hit me like a freight train: my hard-won and beloved career would only last that long. We eventually settled on five years, which was still a system shock, but, of course, "I might be able to pick it up again once our last child left home," maybe *24 years* from now…and in the meantime, my work would be at home with the kids. I was raised *wanting* to stay home with my kids, of course, but it had never occurred to me that that would preclude anything – and everything – else I wanted to do.

I wanted children, of course; we wanted a family together, at the right time, when we were ready. Nothing ever happens quite the way you want it, though, and our first child was a surprise just a couple years in. We were alone in Provo without any extended family nearby, and having a baby was so infinitely much harder than everyone else made it look. I suffered considerable pain, horrendous depression, and other debilitating illnesses cropped up. We went from wanting four kids to wanting one overnight. A year or so later we decided that Child #1 needed to learn to share, had Child #2 ten months later, and when the doctor said my body wouldn't handle another pregnancy, we found ourselves doing the happy dance: We had an excuse to stop breeding! HALLELUJAH!

My children are wonderful. The very best, you see. But we have officially multiplied and replenished the earth, and when you have a "doctor's note" and someone asks you (because they do) why you don't have more children, you can adopt that horribly sad puppy dog look and say "Our doctor won't let us; *it could kill me.*"

Note: Any other reply will deny you sympathy.

I am a stay-home Mormon mom with "just" two kids. I am also a stay-home Mormon mom without a testimony. For those unaware, a "testimony" is a deep and personal belief in the truth of all things LDS, usually a spiritually-driven utterance across the pulpit that sounds something like "I know this church is true, I know that Jesus lived and that Joseph Smith restored His gospel to the earth with the Book of Mormon."

I don't have one of those. *I don't believe it.*

(Yes, I say "I don't believe it" instead of "it's a crock of crap." Tends to go over better. I'd prefer to be honest, but an apostate loses a whole lot of friends in a very short amount of time, so saying "I don't believe it" is self-defense. It mitigates some of the hatred, anger, and resentment, and I'll take what I can get.)

It's been an awfully long road, though. You see, at the end of the book of Moroni, the last book in the Book of Mormon (hereafter referred to as the BoM, a favorite expression of Mormons), Moroni offers a promise in chapter 10, verse 4: "And when ye shall receive these things, I would exhort you that ye would ask God, the Eternal Father, in the name of Christ, if these things are not true; and if ye shall ask with a sincere heart, with real intent, having faith in Christ, he will manifest the truth of it unto you, by the power of the Holy Ghost." Translation: If you've read this far, now you need to pray for a confirmation that this book is the truth, and if you're serious and faithful, God will tell you that it is.

But what if He doesn't?

HE WILL.

Yes, but what if He didn't?

HE PROMISED.

You're not answering my question.

BE PATIENT.

I am.

TRY AGAIN.

…Okay.

At 13 I was a bit more mature than some of my peers…and a great bit more backward in other respects. Point is, I determined to *prove* my faith. I read the BoM from cover to cover – I confess I slacked a little during some of the long and boring "war chapters" – and then got to Moroni 10:4.

Tangent: Did you know what Mark Twain read the BoM? His assessment, and I quote: "Chloroform in print."

I read the verse, and I actually accepted the challenge out loud. I prayed. On my knees. For an hour. Then I knelt there, just listening. For an hour. At 13.

I got nuthin'.

I was distraught, but eventually told myself a) I was too young to really get an answer (after all, Joseph Smith didn't "get an answer" 'til he was 14!) and b) I hadn't read the war chapters with enough real desire or intent. It was *my* fault I hadn't received an answer.

At 15 our seminary class covered the BoM, so during the 8 months of before-school classes, I made sure to read the entire BoM all over again, focusing on every last word. I knelt and prayed. I prayed on and off for days. I got *no* answer…not even a warm, happy feeling. At this point I was *sure* it was my fault, and that I was too great a sinner and too awful a human being to merit a response from God. I needed to change, to improve.

I sought again at 18 during a BoM class at BYU. No answer. I tried again at 19; still no reply. I tried at 21, wondering if God wanted me to serve a mission, unmarried as I was…but since He wouldn't confirm to me that the BoM was true, I wasn't terribly gung-ho about the prospect of a mission. I married at 23, reading the BoM in two weeks, hoping to finally get the answer that marrying in the temple and receiving my endowments was the right thing to do…*after* I'd done them, of course. At no point did God chime in. I gave up for a while, tried at 28, at 29, and finally at 31, giving it "one last shot." Deep down I was so certain that I was worthless and endlessly sinful, and so full of guilt and darkness and treachery, that God didn't love me. He wanted nothing do to with me. I wasn't even worth His time to give me a thumbs' up on the religion I was trying to live to make Him happy.

You can imagine the depression that consumed me.

And I'm not the only one. Utah, of all places in the United States, has one of the highest rates of people on anti-depressants, making them both massively depressed and over-medicated.[i] They're a grand coping mechanism, drugs.

Because you have to cope with things like a local evangelical church showing their young people a muted black-and-white video of Mormon kids doing crazy hand motions, telling their youth that Mormons are brainwashing kids with references to secret temple covenants. *No, people, that's just a creepy-looking video of little church kids learning the silly primary song, "Popcorn Poppin' on the Apricot Tree," teaching them about the pretty white blossoms that pop up in Spring.* And yet you know how you're seen by these people, these neighbors and friends.

You're a freak.

Where's my Prozac?

If I need Prozac when I watch other people's films about Mormons, I need a double dose – and some orange juice – when I watch Mormon propaganda. When I was at BYU the film "The Two Testaments" was all the rage in Salt Lake. It was played in one of the buildings at Temple Square, and I saw it with various groups of friends multiple times, getting a kick out of seeing one of my professors acting in it after I'd had his class. "The Two Testaments" is a back-and-forth movie about Jesus's crucifixion and death, and the "concurrent" happenings in the Americas as Christ was meeting His end. The entire movie is horrible propaganda, and as much as I'd love to go into infinitely more detail about it, suffice it to say that if ever you get a chance to see it, I promise you you'll shudder. I hate the idea that that film could be viewed by anyone outside the church, frankly because it's just so horribly, horribly propagandist…but I digress.

Anytime someone outside the church sees something odd about the church, I find myself on the defensive…still. My favorite incident of total Mormon insanity witnessed by a non-Mormon makes me want to simultaneously laugh and cry to this day. During my freshman year at the Y, a non-Mormon friend from back home also attended the Y; her parents had converted the year before and wanted her to do the same, so they told her they would only pay for college if she went to BYU. (She did not convert, and they reneged on their promise to pay for the couple years she spent there. She still owes over $8,000 for utterly useless units earned.) At the end of our first week she dragged me to her dorm room, closing the door behind us. "Okay, what the hell just happened?" she asked. I had no clue what she was talking about, so she explained: "I was walking through the Wilk [the student center] and there were a bunch of student employees getting one of the ballrooms ready for some dinner. One guy was carrying a stack of plates, but he tripped over something and they all came crashing down and he yelled 'Shit!' and suddenly this girl falls to the floor, puts her arms around her knees in the fetal position and starts rocking back and forth singing 'I am a child of God.' It seriously freaked me out. What, she's never heard anyone say 'shit' before?"

No, my friend. No, she probably hadn't. Not 'til then.

How embarrassing…for Mormons.

We are sort of a joke. We were a joke to a cousin of mine who went with me to Utah to go skiing. We stopped by Temple Square – he'd never seen a Mormon temple before, except on the side of the road in LA and San Diego – and just for kicks he looked up at the temple, waited until a Sister Missionary passed by, grabbed her by the arm (gently) and pointed up to the statue of Moroni at the top. He said (with gusto), "Look at that fucking thing! Look at that giant fucking statue! That's fuckin' amazing!" She patted his hand as she pulled her arm away, smiled charmingly, and disappeared. My cousin roared...and so did I. It was the first time I had been able to really step back and laugh at an outsider's eye roll.

Tangent warning: In Martha Beck's book Leaving the Saints, she notes that she has it on good authority that only the pretty sister missionaries are assigned to Temple Square...the better to ensnare curious young men (and horny old ones!), I guess...

We are not JUST a joke; we are also a *concern*, particularly to born-again Christians. My freshman year at the Y was incredibly difficult, and at its conclusion my high school best friend came for a visit from UC Davis, a notoriously liberal college in Northern California. She was a bit of an enigma there, actually; as a born-again Christian, she represented a more conservative standpoint...whereas at BYU, I seemed to represent a more liberal standpoint, though any Californian would think me ultra-conservative.

I had confided in her some of my concerns about my faith, springing up even then, and she had brought a short story with her that angered me at the time, but I have clung to ever since. In summary, the story told of two families, one LDS and one born-again. The LDS family opts to buy a house, and the born-again family tries to point out that though the home is beautiful, the foundation is termite-ridden. The LDS family buys the home anyway, angry that their friends would point out the home's defects instead of being concerned for the LDS family's well-being, and the home collapses, leaving the born-again family despondent over the loss of their foolish friends.

But my foundation was not rotten! It was TRUE. In fact, there was a hymn at church I used to mentally combat that story, entitled "How Firm a Foundation." And still that story nagged at me, and here I am today finally realizing that rotten roots do not provide good fruit.

I am a skyscraper built on a rotten foundation. I am an apricot that tastes like a prune. I am over-educated in my religion, but I don't know what I'm built on, and now that my blueprint has been destroyed, I'm thinking it's time to rebuild...something.

But what? I've spent 18 months studying the "gospel" with Jehovah's Witnesses, because they're capable of a good conversation...but they're wrong. About a lot of things. I went to a dear friend who is a born-again to ask her about her faith, and to find out why she believes certain things that I was taught were wrong. She doesn't have any answers; she just knows that Jesus saved her. That doesn't help someone like me. I went to another friend's husband, who happens to be a youth pastor at a local Christian church, and I asked him what happens to the little child in Africa who never gets to hear the name of Jesus, who dies, while still a child, of starvation, never knowing someone gave His life to save them. What happens? He looked me in the eye and asked me this: "Why does God have to save that child? Did you ever consider that some people weren't meant to be saved?"

No. I hadn't considered that. It is now time to run screaming for the door, thanks.

At one point I went out with a dear friend who is Catholic, and who I credit to some degree with keeping me from suicide in high school. We didn't discuss religion much, but she bought me my very first Strawberry Blonde beer. Of all the moments of my life concerning my, versus someone else's, religion, this was the best exchange ever: the Catholic buying the Mormon a beer. I didn't convert to Catholicism, but I sure was grateful for her willingness to allow me a new experience, sans judgment.

I have sought and searched, studied world religions, and I have pursued and continue to pursue knowledge and truth, whether I like what anyone has to say or not. My husband does the same. One day we were sitting in church, and he pulled out a piece of paper and a pen and started jotting down all sorts of calculations and percentages, and drawing pie charts and graphs. I waited as patiently as I could, and finally my patience was rewarded: he leaned over and presented me with his conclusions. His charts and graphs showed how many people were Mormon, what approximate percentage of those were "active" and "worthy", and how many people throughout time had "had their work done for them" – had been vicariously baptized and had ordinances performed on their behalf that they could choose to accept or ignore up in heaven – and what percentage of those people might have accepted the work performed. He then divided that number by the likely number of people who have lived on the earth, careful to point out that all estimates were conservative. Ultimately he discovered that, of all the "sons and daughters of God" who have lived on the earth thus far, only approximately 0.004% would "make it" to the Celestial Kingdom, or, according to Mormons, back to the highest degree of Heaven to live with God the Father. Next to his charts and graphs were a few short sentences under the heading "Conclusion":

1. God doesn't expect many of His children to make it back.
2. God's plan for mankind is unreasonable and generally unattainable.
3. Mormons misunderstand God's plan for mankind.

I circled number 3, we shrugged grumpily, and went back to our respective thoughts, but his chart stuck with me. When a friend's wife asked him to read Fawn Brodie's <u>No Man Knows My History</u>, a biography of Joseph Smith, founder of the LDS faith, and I reflected on my husband's musings, I wondered why I shouldn't allow myself to read it, too. If the gospel was true, wouldn't it hold up to scrutiny? Our friend had only gotten a few chapters in, but I was ready to hear what someone else had to say. We're told we should stay away from "anti-Mormon literature," of course, but Brodie started out a Mormon and was excommunicated for what she found because *she was unwilling to change what she had written about her discovery.* Could there be enough out there that I, too, after uncovering the bulk of it, would believe otherwise? Brodie's book is a big one, well-written and cross-referenced, thorough and full of footnotes, her personal opinions easily separated from her careful disclosure of facts. *How much information could there really be to disprove Mormonism?* I wondered. I gave it a shot. I read it cover to cover, weeping most of the time. ALL my questions were answered.

I felt like Eve in the Garden of Eden: *My eyes had been opened.* I had been lied to. Worse, I had spent decades living my life for those lies, trying to fashion myself into a being that conformed to the standard of those lies. My wakeup call was no ringing phone; it was brass knuckles to the chin.

The worst night of my life was when we brought our first child home from the hospital with jaundice so severe that our baby was forced to sleep in a bili-light suitcase. I, having just had a c-section, was in great pain, partially delirious, and very drugged. I was used to our child crying every couple hours. When I fell asleep, the baby did not wake me, and I awoke with a start realizing our child had remained silent (in my mind) "far too long." I leapt from the couch and found him (sound asleep, but what I believed was) dead in the open suitcase. I scooped up the baby, felt for a pulse that I could not find, apologized to my child as I sobbed uncontrollably, and lay on the floor with my (sleeping) babe on my chest because I could not figure out how to stand back up. Minutes (days?) later my husband swooped in, snatched the baby (even as I raved that I had killed it), and, after explaining that our child was NOT, in fact, dead, he sent me to bed, where I ultimately collapsed.

I relate that awful story because there is only one other night in my life that vies for the title of Worst Night of My Life: the night it dawned on me that Mormonism was a farce.

After the first 200 pages of <u>No Man Knows My History</u> I set the book down, turned to my husband, and tried to explain what I had just learned: that Joseph Smith was a charlatan and that the Book of Mormon was unequivocally NOT TRUE. I couldn't, however, use those words, a) because I was still in denial, and b) because when you tell a Mormon that you no longer believe, that's exactly what you say. "I no longer believe." Not, "It's all bullshit." Besides, he'd read none of what I just had. He knew nothing about any of what I now understood. Simply, he didn't know what he didn't know, and I was loathe to tell him.

I sobbed for 2 ½ solid hours that night. I cried myself sick and exhausted; in fact, I had no idea I could have that many tears to shed. I could not function, and though my sweet husband did his best to comfort me, there was no comfort to be had. If I could have stood back from the situation to see it for what it was, I'd have watched my world unravel around me. Authority and trust, friendship and family, who I was, where I came from, where I'm headed, my very nature – not a literal daughter of God, but a common human being – everything evaporated, all at once.

<u>EVERYTHING I'D EVER KNOWN</u> – I don't know how to write that with more emphasis – had be eradicated by the fact that the Book of Mormon was a fraud.

200 pages of a 500 page biography was all it took for me to FINALLY understand that the answer I'd so desperately desired would never, ever come. Like the night I believed I had killed my own child, I suffered from abject despair. Unless you've been there yourself, it really is difficult to imagine what that's like.

(Since then, I've discovered that the rabbit hole only goes deeper, that it may be never ending, and that I have been the worst possible indoctrinated dupe for my entire life.)

By the next day, resentment had flooded in. I stood back and looked at my life, at the blueprint that had been handed to me during childhood that I had built myself around: baptism, a young women's medallion (the churchy female equivalent of an Eagle Scout), seminary (four years' intensive early-morning scriptural studies during high school), a BYU degree, a temple marriage, children I was raising to be Mormon, a marriage in shambles due to the trio of my husband's bishopric callings, horrible work hours, and my depression, and I had the most amazing image come to mind…one that I don't actually believe to be correct, but a telling image, nonetheless.

I pictured the Prophet and his presidency with all twelve apostles sitting around a big white conference table in an upper room of the Salt Lake Temple, leaning back in their chairs with lit stogies and brandy snifters in hand, all having a good laugh.

At my expense.

(Speaking of stogies, who knew that Willard Richards, one of the "apostles" in Carthage Jail alongside Joseph Smith when Joseph met his end, attained a cigar courtesy of the Prophet Joseph "to calm him stomach"? It was news to me! Frankly, it'd probably be news to most devout Mormons, too!)

Since childhood I've imagined the Prophet in that same Upper Room kneeling before the physical Lord Jesus Christ, listening humbly to the things the Lord would have the Prophet reveal to His people during the next General Conference of the Church. Now I was picturing him drunk, fellating a cigar, watching the tithing dollars roll in while I figuratively whipped myself with a cat-o'-nine-tails for not reading my scriptures regularly enough.

Meanwhile I have friends leaving the church, even as I'm busy berating myself for my inadequacies. No, I'm not perfect – *far from it* – but I'm not a "bad" person. At the same time, people for whom I care very much are leaving their guilt and worthlessness behind them and moving on…and I am *devastated* for their sakes? I had introduced a friend of mine in high school to the church, the same born-again best friend who came to visit me at the Y after freshman year, and I was inconsolable when she decided not to join. One of my siblings had left the church after only a short stint at BYU in Idaho, and I remember how despondent I was, thinking her *lost*. She wasn't suffering over my fears; *I* was. She wasn't still beating herself for her "sins"; *I* was. She was happy.

I wasn't.

If I could be so devastated over my friend not joining, my other friends leaving, and my own sister walking away, how would people handle *my* leaving the church? Would they be devastated over me? Would they, like Ann-Eliza Webb (a wife of Brigham Young)'s mother when she left the church, tell me that they had rather I had died? (She really did. Really.)

And then I imagined what would happen if the church were PROVED fraudulent, or, unimaginably, they came clean. What if instead of announcing to the world that 18 year-old boys could now serve missions (as President Monson did in the October 2012 General Conference), they came out and said, "We did our best, but we finally realized that Joseph Smith and Brigham Young were full of poo, and we just can't keep up their charade."

NO.

SERIOUSLY.

THINK ABOUT IT.

What would happen? Would people still cling to it? Would our missionaries burn BoMs in the streets? Would LDS faithful be found at home in their bathtubs having slit their wrists, or would they be crawling up the front steps of other churches on their hands and knees begging for answers? Would elderly LDS folk keep up their temple visits and pretend they hadn't heard?

What would happen if the Mormon Church came clean?

To answer that, you first have to know what it's like to be a Mormon.

Buckle your seatbelt.

What it's Like to be Mormon

My freshman year at Brigham Young University I, like most other freshmen, took Book of Mormon 101. On day two of class I got there early – probably the first, last, and only time I ever showed up to a college class early – and, having been thrown for a loop when I moved from multicultural Southern California to mostly-white Happy Valley, I sat down next to the only tan girl in the room: a Muslim from Saudi Arabia. She was lovely, lonely, and wrapped in religious garb so that the only evidence that her skin was any darker than bleached all-purpose flour was her face. She was just as surprised that I sat with her as I was that there was a Muslim girl taking a BoM class. We chatted, and she was delightful. Finally I asked the obvious: "If you're Muslim, what on earth are you doing *here*?"

Her reply was very telling, though I was too young at the time to process it: "My parents wanted me to attend University in America, but this is the only college with values similar to ours where they felt I would be safe."

Many years later (and thanks, in part, to Kay Burningham) it has finally dawned on me: If you want to know what it's like to be a Mormon, and you have any background at all with Islam, *you already know what it's like to be a Mormon.* (Note: a friend told me that the following comparison is a little irrelevant to this book and that I'm being a bit presumptuous, imagining that I know what it's like to be a Muslim, but I've chosen to leave it in because I feel it's a rather eye-opening link. You be the judge.) Consider the following: am I describing what it's like to be a Muslim, or a Mormon? The answer is unequivocally BOTH.

1. The religion was instituted by a man named Mohammed/Joseph Smith, who claimed to have been sent as a prophet by God to restore the truth of all things in their entirety, once and for all time, through the Qu'ran/Book of Mormon.
2. The religion claims to be God's final word in all things; for additional questions, please see the Imams/Brethren.
3. The faith has created a sort of Theocracy for its people.

Believers support the government so long as the government does what the religious leaders say God wants, and believers desire that governmental leaders be members of their faith.

4. The faith is a form of religious ethnocentrism. God favors the faith's membership above all people and has blessed them accordingly.

5. The religion features an extreme form of patriarchy in which the woman is subject to the man and his decisions are final. All general and local leadership positions are filled by men, ostensibly with the power to speak on behalf of God.

6. The faith is practiced in special buildings called mosques/ temples set aside for the worship of God wherein the sexes sit separately for services.

7. The belief reaffirms the relevancy, necessity, and beauty of polygamy.

8. The faith has a specific dress code, most of which revolves around culturally-extreme modesty standards for women.

9. The religion has practiced – or continues to practice – blood atonement, including death to apostates and infidels, and extreme punishment for various sins.

10. Lest we forget, both religions are based in a big desert.

In this modern age, the above bits and bobs are how I was raised. There was a running joke in our home when I was young: Dad was married before Mom, but the marriage didn't last. His ex-wife got the dog, but they had no kids, so other than some mild bitterness over a well-trained pooch, Dad was okay making his exit. When people learned we were Mormon and would ask – *yes, they did!* – how many wives my Dad had, Dad would say "Two. But I divorced the first before I married the second."

And knowing Mom, polygamy would *not* have gone over in our household.

But other stuff did. Upon turning 12, a young woman (in my case) moves up from Primary (the kids' group) to Young Women's. Every two years from there you move up to a different class: at 12 & 13, you're a Beehive. At 14 & 15, you become a Mia Maid. During your 16th and 17th years, you're a Laurel. (None of us are really sure why those are our titles, but even if we were to ask, I'm not sure anyone would have an answer.) At

12, as a Beehive, you're handed a pamphlet to welcome you into the young women's program. It's entitled "For the Strength of Youth," and it details all the things you can and should be doing to follow the Lord's will for you.

And it threw me for a loop.

If you go to lds.org and search for "strength of youth", you'll find it immediately. It's worth a thorough read, but I just want to cover the highlights as relevant to my 12 year-old self. And so...things to do and not to do at TWELVE: (Please remember, these "suggestions" are taken VERY seriously by members of the church and are meant to help young people, not horrify adults.)

1. You should not date until you are at least 16 years old; go with one or more couples and avoid going on frequent dates with the same person, which can perhaps lead to immorality. Remember that a young man and a young woman on a date are responsible to protect each other's honor and virtue. As you enter adult years, make dating and marriage a high priority. Marrying in the temple and creating an eternal family are essential in God's plan of happiness.

2. Immodest clothing is clothing that is tight, sheer, or revealing in any other manner. Young women should avoid short shorts and short skirts, shirts that do not cover the stomach, and clothing that does not cover the shoulders or is low cut in the front or back. Do not disfigure yourself with tattoos or body piercings. If you desire to have your ears pierced, wear only one pair of earrings.

3. Select only media that uplifts you. Avoid pornography at all costs. Attend only those dances where dress, grooming, lighting, lyrics, music, and entertainment contribute to a wholesome atmosphere where the Spirit can be present.

4. Do not use profane, vulgar, or crude language or gestures, and do not tell jokes or stories about immoral actions. These are offensive to God and to others.

5. Do not drink coffee or tea. Never use tobacco products or any form of alcohol. Avoid any drink, drug, chemical, or dangerous practice that is used to produce a high; some of these include marijuana, hard drugs, prescription or over-the-

counter medications that are abused, or household chemicals.

6. Before marriage, do not participate in passionate kissing, lie on top of another person, or touch the private, sacred parts of another person's body, with or without clothing. Do not do anything else that arouses sexual feelings. Do not arouse those emotions in your own body. The Spirit of the Lord will withdraw from one who is in sexual transgression.

7. Paying tithing is a sacred privilege. Your attitude is important in paying tithing. Pay it first, even when you do not think you have enough money to meet your other needs. [Note: I still struggle with the idea that this is in a YOUTH PAMPHLET.]

Mind you, there are loads of other things in the pamphlet, and it's phrased a bit different from the way they phrased it when I was young (which, by the way, would have saved me a LOT of confusion at 12!), but you get the gist. Most of it is positive and uplifting, "God loves you, show Him love back!" kind of stuff...but at 12, we're already focused on marriage. At 12, with a body that isn't anywhere near "womanly" yet, we're already being told to cover up. (Men are told to be modest, too, but they aren't handed the above-listed guidelines.) At 12, we're imagining the sorts of dances that *don't* fit the Mormon mold and wondering what exactly pornography looks like. By this time we're feeling guilty because we've already started saying "hell", and now we're going there as a result. We've been inundated by D.A.R.E. 'til now, but suddenly my non-member Grandma is evil for her Sweet Tea and I'm thinking of reporting Mom to the bishop (a la Hitler Youth) because she "overuses" Vicodin. (Doesn't she? I mean, she takes it sometimes. Isn't that overuse?) In the version I was handed at 12, we were told not to engage in "masturbation," not just to "not arouse those emotions in our own bodies." I didn't know what masturbation was, and when the light bulb went on I thought, "WHAT?! That's wrong?! Great, now I'm definitely going to hell!" (Stopping was not an option, clearly.) And at 12 I was told to pay tithing first, even when my money was insufficient to meet my *real* needs.

The church gets you young, and they keep getting you.

You memorize the Young Women's Theme, recited every Sunday before classes, and every time (once a week, usually Wednesday night) that Mutual is held (the young men's and young women's groups get together for an activity): "We are daughters of our Heavenly Father, who loves us, and we love Him. We will stands as witnesses of God at all times and in all things and in all places as we strive to live the Young Women Values, which are: Faith, Divine Nature, Individual Worth, Knowledge, Choice and Accountability, Good Works, and Integrity ['and Virtue', the newest one]. We believe as we come to accept and act upon these values, we will be prepared to make and keep sacred covenants, receive the ordinances of the temple, and enjoy the blessings of exaltation."

Yup, still memorized.

You attend 3 hours of meetings on Sunday, Mutual on Wednesday night, and seminary in the morning, of course, but there are other "righteous pursuits" you have to fit into your spiritual – and secular – calendar: nowadays lots of stakes (on the local level, we meet in wards, multiple wards make a stake, stakes make a region, and so on) hold "Trek", a 2-3 day pioneer-style handcart-pulling hike over rough terrain (where you're broken into "family" groups and bond over hard labor and gospel reliance to repeat the pioneers' difficulties). Every stake has Girls' Camp each summer for about 5 days: *all gospel, all the time.* You might be in a class presidency and have to attend presidency meetings to organize activities for your class, and attend Bishop's Youth Committee if you're a class president, which is another hour on Sunday once a month. There are temple trips to do baptisms for the dead, visits to newly-built temples to experience the pre-dedication walk-through (and picture yourself preparing for your wedding day in the bride's room) and, of course, you only have 6 years to pass off a huge number of journal entries, conversations, and service projects in order to receive your Young Women's Medallion, the necklace equivalent of a spiritual Eagle Scout award.

In other words, as a young woman in the LDS church, you are completely inundated and smothered by the emotional-hormonal-spiritual musings and expectations of your peers, leaders and parents.

It's not all that great to be a guy, either. Boys are supposed to be ready and worthy to receive the Aaronic (not quite so magical, lesser) priesthood at 12 and to progress in the priesthood at 14 and 16, meaning at 16 they could technically baptize someone! (Provided, of course, they abstain from masturbation!) By 8 or 9 they've already been thrust into Cub and then Boy Scouts, and by the time they graduate from high school, they're expected to have earned both their Eagle Scout (which looks much better on a resume than, say, a YW Medallion) and their Duty to God award, an above-and-beyond religious scouting award from the church.

To support a young woman in getting her medallion, you may be asked to serve in the YW organization at some point…maybe…if you're a woman. To support the boys in becoming Eagle Scouts, however, you may get called to be troop mom, pack leader, what-have-you, even though you don't have any boys in the program. (A dear friend, who has a 5 year-old son, has been a den mother for 2 years now, even though it's a disaster to try to fit it into her schedule.) Additionally, Friends of Scouting comes 'round every year, which equates to some member of the priesthood or bishopric emailing/calling/knocking on your door to ask you to contribute "generously" to "Friends of Scouting." Yes, above and beyond the already-required 10% of your gross income and a generous "fast offering" every first Sunday of the month. (Apparently scouting is far more expensive than the activities enjoyed by the young women.)

But to jump back to masturbating, I remember the moment I discovered I was *evil*: my mother explained to me what masturbation meant when I asked about the Strength of Youth pamphlet.

I was shocked. I was horrified. I was GUILT-LADEN, and I really did determine then and there to stop…forever. I wasn't about to confess my sin because I just couldn't bear, at 12, to walk into the bishop's office and confess to the innocent discovery of my clitoris and the amazing thing it did. Instead, I cracked open President Kimball's humdinger of a guilt trip called The Miracle of Forgiveness (also known as "The book that should never be read by a new missionary unless he wants to feel so guilty for his existence that he'll end up leaving his mission") and attempted to put into practice some of the Brethren's suggestions to avoid masturbation. These ranged from wearing tight (but not *too* tight!) pajamas and constricting underclothing (obviously written more for boys than girls), to sleeping with your door open, to singing children's hymns out loud and even *calling or visiting with your family members to help distract you from your evil desires.*

Does anyone else find that unnervingly Oedipal?

Needless to say, none of the Brethren's advice did much for me, and after 3 years, I still hadn't confessed to my sins. Then came a temple trip for baptisms. I attended, but LIED to the bishop when he interviewed me to determine my temple-worthiness. On the Sunday before we went to the temple, one of my young women's teacher's decided to teach an Old Testament lesson about how someone tried to go into the temple unworthily and God struck them DEAD.

I realize that this is humorous, but once you've finished laughing, please take a step back and look at this story again from my 15 year-old point of view…from the view of one who had been indoctrinated by the Mormon Church since birth:

I knew that God struck dead those who were unworthy of entering the temple but entered anyway. I also knew that I lacked the courage to tell the bishop I was an evil chronic masturbator (read: a couple times a week) who has succumbed to temptation. I knew that I *had* to go to the temple, because to *not* go to the temple would show the rest of the world that I was evil, and I was afraid of what sins they'd suspect I had engaged in. So what did I do? I hugged and kissed my parents and siblings, trying desperately not to choke up before I left to visit the Los Angeles temple, *knowing full well I would never see any of them again.* I would be *struck dead* the moment I tried to enter the temple, and I would *deserve it.* God could not permit evil inside His Holy Home, and since I lacked the courage to repent, I would reap my reward: DEATH. Not only would I never see my family again in this life, because of my wickedness, I would not see them in any sort of afterlife, either.

I…was…doomed.

We got to the temple, I blotted my eyes, squared up my shoulders, and held it together pretty well. I remember a young women's leader patting me on the back and handing me another tissue, assuming I was so moved by the experience of being at the temple that I was weeping uncontrollably. (By then I really was weeping uncontrollably.) Still I pressed forward, and it was my turn to plunge through the temple door…

And nothing happened. I was still there, my peers were still pushing through behind me and spreading out in front of me, and when the man behind the front desk at the temple read my name aloud and I stepped forward to identify myself, I was sure THAT would be it…and then he waved me through to follow my peers on down to the baptismal font.

THAT RIGHT THERE was my very first inclination that maybe, perhaps, possibly, just *maybe* my religion *might not* be true. Why?

BECAUSE GOD DID NOT SMITE ME.

Please pardon my penchant for the dramatic. I think it's just characteristic of Mormonism.

*   *   *

We Mormons have a very "Us versus Them" mentality, and nowhere is that more visible than in Utah. It's like any group who perceives themselves ridiculed, marginalized, or just generally hated: Mormons seem to feel camaraderie with other persecuted peoples, even if those same peoples feel little or no camaraderie with us. We love to point out that we are the only group in these United States that have ever been the subject of an order of genocide, and that, thanks to an angry liberal Hollywood, we are constantly harassed, our most sacred things made into public jokes by "Big Love" and Broadway's "The Book of Mormon" shows.

And yet we ENDURE.

I think the best way to describe it is to call it a skewed superiority complex: we are ridiculed and reviled because we are RIGHT, RIGHTEOUS, and CALLED TO SUFFER. (People notoriously think of Jews this way, another "chosen people," though I think Mormons are far more obsessive about their perceived sufferings…this century, and last!)

The Doctrine and Covenants (hereafter referred to as the D&C), another book of Mormon scripture comprised of modern-day revelations given directly through Joseph Smith, says the following in section 82:3: "For of him unto whom much is given, much is required." Mormons have been given "everything", which means, in turn, we are required to "give" more than most other people. We're special. We *know* more, and so we're responsible to *do* more. We are *blessed*. We need to show gratitude for our blessings to the degree that we've been blessed, which blessings are infinite.

We are blessed with everything, we know everything, and we're special. (Sounds like what's wrong with American kids today, doesn't it?)

I think it's been a few paragraphs since I embarrassed myself, so allow me, if you will, to do so again. Last year a dear friend of mine invited me to her birthday party with her family. She was a couple months pregnant, and she and her husband chose that day to announce the pregnancy to her father and step-mother, and I was invited to be present for the announcement. Her parents were obviously delighted, and her father, who is at least my own father's age and a born-again Christian, asked that the 5 of us offer up a prayer of gratitude to God for this great blessing. We gathered in a circle, held one another's hands, and he offered a prayer that went something like this:

"Dear God, We come to you to thank you for this amazing blessing of another grandbaby on the way. We are so delighted that in just a few months we'll be welcoming this child into our family, and we just want you to know that we love you, that we're so grateful, and that we hope you'll be with my daughter as she carries this precious baby. God, we just love you, and we're so thankful. In Jesus's name, Amen."

What did I do? I tried not to roll my eyes, thinking how sweet it was – *in the most condescending way* – that he would want to stop and pray, but how unfortunate that he just didn't understand the *proper* way to pray. In other words, I listened to the earnest, heartfelt prayer of a grateful man as he poured out his devotion and love to the God with whom he has built a personal relationship and judged that relationship wanting based on his "ignorance" of the "fact" that he *should* have been more formal in his address. (Mormons pray with "Dear Heavenly Father, we thank thee, we ask thee, in the name of Thy Son," etc.)

Really, who the hell did I think I was to set myself above a man twice my age, believing my understanding of God's expectations superior to his? What a chump!

I experienced a similar situation recently, from the perspective of my friend's father. I had put a comment on facebook about being horrified by the truth of polygamy, and a college kid (currently enrolled at the Y) chimed in with a painfully condescending response to my disgust, explaining what every Mormon college kid is taught to believe regarding polygamy: that it occurred in less than 2% of the population and that the men engaging in it had to be "called of God" and "righteous." He actually mentioned Ann-Eliza Webb (though not by name) as the one wife who divorced Brigham ("who begged to be a wife of his then demanded her own house", and I quote) but suggested SHE was the problem (SORRY, ANN-ELIZA!). Finally he stated the following: "When obedience ceases to be a burden and becomes a quest, in that moment we are endowed with power from on high." He's 22, profoundly self-righteous (like I once was), and has no idea what life experiences could possibly have led me away from being "endowed with power from on high."

But he was taught those things, just as I was, and will defend them to the death, just like I would have. Even though none of what he had to say was actually true, he believes it is. Firmly.

Ever heard of Cognitive Dissonance? I remember having heard the term once or twice, probably in a psychology class, but until I started really delving into my beliefs (and whether or not I truly believed them), I never related cognitive dissonance to myself. Now I see it in every single part of me, and it scares me to death to see what I've become.

What is Cognitive Dissonance? It has a few inter-related definitions, and it relates to many groups, most religious, but not just Mormons. In fact, you may be unlucky enough to find yourself in one of the following definitions:

1. The emotionally-disabling state of holding two contradictory or conflicting ideas, beliefs, or values simultaneously.
2. The tendency, driven by uncomfortable feelings, to *repel* or to *justify* contradictory information.
3. The uneasy feeling that drives the mind to *explain* and/or *lie* and/or *separate from* logical contradiction.

Interestingly, I've discovered that cognitive dissonance has a sort of crescendo effect, meaning that the bigger and stronger the belief invested in a particular claim, the more devotedly those of us with CD (illogically) dismiss or refute that claim. Take, for instance, God hearing prayers. As a Mormon, I'm absolutely certain that He hears my prayers. Along comes an atheist, who points out that your average church-goer receives answers to prayers about as often as an atheist would find a solution to a particular problem. Maybe, when we say that sometimes prayers are answered "the way we want," but sometimes "God says no," what's really happening is that sometimes problems have a solution, and sometimes they don't.

What does the Mormon reply? Depending on how intensely I believe God hears my prayers, I will a) dismiss what they have to say as coming from someone who "just doesn't get it." I could also b) defer my argument to an expert, ie. "President Hinckley said…" which is incredibly common in the LDS church, conditioned as we are to "follow the prophet" and "honor the priesthood." Finally, I could c) justify my claim about prayer by explaining any number of illogical-but-rationalized things, from "God loves atheists, too," to "God answers on His own timetable," to "God hears *all* prayers –we know because He said so! – but He doesn't have to *answer* them."

In other words, with CD, while following options a), b), or c) may help us to dismiss our spiritual discomfort, the problem hasn't actually be rectified. The atheist's argument still stands, and somewhere in the back of our minds, if we are in any way still rational people, it freaks us out.

We may no longer be rational people, however. The amount of conditioning that goes into an entire lifetime when you're raised in an active Mormon family is generally pretty extreme. Consider, if you will, the bulk of evidence available (particularly via the internet!) to debunk the LDS faith, and that most members, though warned against "anti-Mormon literature," have come across it at some point. Yet those of us who are aware of the evidence against the faith and still believe the church is true are not willing to impartially analyze the evidence. Why? Because of the lasting effects of LDS conditioning. (In the church we actually call it "anti-Mormon literature." Can you *be* more conditioned?) (Or more Us vs. Them, for that matter???)

So then there's me. I was conditioned. I believed to the best of my ability, but something always nagged at the back of my mind. It makes me wonder if there is something deep in my brain, some little subconscious mechanism that functions like a warning sign, flashing every time I come up against something illogical. It has taken years of conditioning to repress that mechanism, and considerable soul-searching to even recognize that it may exist, but unless it does exist – unless there really is a warning signal in my brain that goes off when I'm faced with illogical things – could I have broken free of decades of conditioning? And how long has that warning signal been flashing? How long have I been fighting it? How many unsettled issues have been piling up inside my head all these years?

Why did it take me so long to yell "ENOUGH!"?

Because I'm a Mormon. Or at least, I was. But I digress. More on what that's like.

One of the things at church that always created cognitive dissonance for me – though I had no idea that that's what it was – was the act of sustaining a calling. In the church, callings are extended to various individuals in the general membership, from "Ward Greeter" (yes, that really is a calling in some places!) to Primary President to Bishop to Relief Society Pianist to Nursery Worker and everything in between. Ostensibly, those callings come from God. The bishop is "told" by God (or receives some sort of inspiration or impression) that a particular person should be extended a particular calling, and that individual is then called to serve in that capacity. In church the following Sunday, the calling is announced to the ward, the person stands, and the entire ward "votes" the person into the calling by a raise of the right hand, called "sustaining". They ask "all those in favor" to raise their hand, and then ask for "any opposed" to do the same, though no one ever raises a hand. (I remember raising my hand proudly as a tiny little girl, and my parents pulling down my arm and giving me a look when I innocently "opposed" whoever was receiving a calling right then.) Even if you *knew* the person getting the calling was a child molester and should be publicly hamstringed instead of given a calling to, say, teach a Primary class, you *never* raise your hand as one "opposed."

After all, their calling came from God, didn't it?

I remember in high school a kid was called to be leader of the Priest's quorum, the group of 16 and 17 year-old boys. I knew *from his girlfriend* that he and she had been having sex for over a year. I raised my hand to sustain him, but sought a few moments with the bishop afterward to give him the heads' up. "Well, why did you sustain him, then?" asked the bishop.

The boy remained in the calling.

Things like that create some serious doubt that callings come directly from God. Personally I believe that, more often than not, they're *not* divinely inspired; callings come from *convenience*. When your ward is 400 – or 800! – people strong, there's a lot to be done, and only so many people willing to do it. Then there are the people who are willing, but won't be called because they aren't deemed "up to snuff." A brother we know didn't serve a mission, and to this day he has never had a calling outside of Primary. A sister and her husband married outside the temple, and neither have ever served in any major capacity, either, though they've now been sealed and all of their children were born in the covenant. Let's face it: if calls were divinely inspired, I would be handing out programs on Sunday.

But that's not what happens.

We moved into a ward and were immediately assigned to speak in sacrament meeting a few weeks later, and having been an Arts major, I carry myself well. Having received a BA, I can write an essay with the best of them. Having taught school, I have the ability to stand in front of a classroom and "perform" a lesson plan. The gospel doctrine teacher moved out of state one week after we spoke in church, and the bishop assured me that "I had been called of God" to be the new gospel doctrine teacher.

Far from it. With a seriously wavering testimony and tons of time to comb through facts and history, calling me to teach the Old Testament was not in my best interest, but it was incredibly convenient for the bishopric to have someone to fill their vacancy.

I'm fairly certain that *God* doesn't want *me* teaching Mormons about their faith. (He'd rather have the brother who replaced me when I asked to be released: Brother Disco Ball. I kid you not, this brother was notorious for his object lessons, one of which was an elaborate disco ball and lights – plus stadium-style seating! – *thing*, and another involving a giant glass water dispenser and some food color. I realize I'm repeating myself, but *I kid you not!*)

I'm also certain that the bishop and his counselors a) knew my background, b) heard me give a phenomenal, memorized, artsy-fartsy "spiritual" talk and were impressed, and c) knew I'd taught gospel doctrine before at the Y, which is letter d) I *went* to the Y, and e), lest we forget, I'm a married-in-the-temple stay-home mom. (That's like extra credit!) If the credentials line up with the calling and the time is right, chances are you'll wind up in a calling that matches your credentials. (If you end up being called to teach your own kid's class, be assured it is because your child is a *living terror*, in which case your call was neither divine nor convenient; it was a war stratagem.)

Experiences like boy-banging-girlfriend also create some serious social hang-ups in the church. While you're meant to feel like part of a ward "family" where everyone loves and is looking out for you, more often than not you feel like a member of the Hitler Youth, assigned to turn in your family members as appropriate. (It's *far* worse at BYU, but we'll get to that later.) After all, do you want your 12 year-old daughter taught the Word of Wisdom by a closet coffee ice cream eater? Or your convert friend in a gospel essentials class taught by a garment-shirker? What about your mother instructed in Relief Society by a swinger? These things do go on, and though God may know about them, the bishop doesn't always. It's *your* job to keep him updated.

Suffice it to say, SOCIAL HANG-UPS.

Being a Mormon means, too, that there is no moderation. Everything is black and white. You either *can* do it, or you *can't* do it. "For the

Strength of Youth" used to be much more specific about "can's and can'ts", and in the sexual purity section the can'ts were spelled out in much greater detail.

Because clearly, if you don't spell it out, a Mormon kid used to having everything spelled out will find exceptions! If it says no "heavy petting," does that mean not under clothes, but above is okay? Or under, but up top and not below? Or maybe not at all, in which case, does accidentally brushing against someone's backside while dancing qualify as petting, and do you have to talk to the bishop about it? If there's no passionate kissing, does that preclude tongues? Is there a time limit, and passing that limit means you've crossed over into passionate kissing? Can you nibble someone's ear? And what about necks? No one ever said anything about necks! (Or was that stated somewhere below as "no necking," and what exactly does "necking" entail?)

We, as Mormons, are so accustomed to having things specifically spelled out for us that we struggle making our own determinations. Gray areas *terrify* us.

One of those gray areas is caffeine.

You may laugh, but it's a struggle.

As a Mormon, we adhere to the Word of Wisdom, a sort of Mormon dietary law listed in the D&C that was given to Joseph Smith directly from God. (At least, we pretend to adhere to it. Like so many in America, a visit to a ward building on Sunday will show that perhaps a good 50% of Mormons are obese, so we're not paying all that much attention to the "do this" part, like "eat foods in their season" and "eat more fruits, veggies, and whole grains with limited meat", or even "early to bed and early to rise," though it's not phrased exactly that way, not to worry.)

On the Word of Wisdom list of don'ts:

1. Coffee (including decaffeinated coffee)
2. Tea (black, green…anything but herbal, which has been deemed just fine) (Note: green tea is now justifiable, thanks to the church's continuing attempts to convert Asians.)
3. Alcohol (preferably not in food, either, if something else can be substituted)
4. Tobacco (chewing and/or smoking)
5. Illegal drugs (including prescription drugs taken improperly)

There's really nothing wrong with that list either way, of course; lots of people are addicted to any or all of those substances, and addiction stinks. I'm fairly certain (outside of where the Word of Wisdom originated from, which is bunk) that it's a good idea to stay away from some of those things entirely, and others if you have a genetic propensity for addiction. That said, allow me to regale you with a story straight from one of my gospel doctrine classes:

After covering the basics of the Word of Wisdom (and I having chosen to focus on the "do's" this time around), Brother A raised his hand to point out that the Brethren have never been clear on the subject of caffeinated sodas, and asks if I have any input for him. Brother B raised his hand, stating "I have an answer to that!" I deferred to Brother B, who explained that yes, in fact, President Hinckley *had* made a comment "a few years back" in a television interview stating that we do, in fact, abstain from caffeinated soda.

Suddenly, a Brother C began waving his hand madly in the air from the back of the room, and I knew this was going to get good.

I called on Brother C, who turned to Brother B and informed him that the Prophet had misspoken, admitting as much in some talk-or-other sometime later, and that the Prophet had been speaking as one of the general membership, not as Prophet. Therefore Brother C still felt justified in drinking the occasional Coke.

This offended the living hell out of Brother B, who, ignoring that a teacher was present in the room to direct discussion, proceeded to call Brother C a sinner and told him he was misleading the entire group and encouraging them to follow after Satan in their soda-cision-making. At this point I caught my husband's eye, and he disappeared from the room.

Sister D piped in, angry that self-righteous Brother B could so cavalierly call Brother C – and those like him, which Sister D was – a sinner when she, too, felt perfectly comfortable enjoying a Dr. Pepper once in a while.

Brother B insisted he meant no offense, but that here, too, was another member leading the fold away from the true gospel, which gospel, he was certain, intended to deny us our Coke. "After all, why are we told not to drink coffee and tea? Because people get addicted to the caffeine! Just because you two are strong enough not to get addicted to your soft drinks doesn't mean that – " *I kid you not, he pointed to his wife!* "– Sister

B has the same sort of willpower!"

In walked my wonderful, sexy, amazing husband with the bishop on his heels.

Oh, our dear Bishop. I would not wish bishop-hood on my worst enemy, let alone anyone for whom I cared. (We'll get to that.)

The bishop walked in, put his hands in the air, and said, "Brothers and sisters, I think this conversation is missing the point." Brothers B & C opened their mouths, but Bishop raised his hand and continued: "To the best of my knowledge, the Church has withheld an opinion about caffeinated sodas. We are therefore left to judge whether or not we personally feel comfortable partaking, within the realms of our individual testimonies. If you *do* feel comfortable participating in such activities, please do not place a stumbling block before your brothers and sisters by proclaiming that they, too, should partake. However, if you are convinced that you yourself should *not* partake of such substances, please do not place a stumbling block before your brothers and sisters by proclaiming their sinful nature when, in fact, the church takes no stance on caffeinated sodas."

That ended the conversation, and I went home later that day not sure whether to laugh at the lunacy of the whole thing, or cry because of it.

So, that's the Word of Wisdom. Ever heard of the Articles of Faith? It's a listing of 13 things Mormons believe wholeheartedly. I think we need to add a 14th: "We believe everything is black and white; that the concept of moderation in all things, though Biblical, is insufficient to guide the Saints in these latter days." It'd fit.

It would fit because there are lots *more* things in our lives the church controls. If you are a Mormon, you know full well that you should not – *must not!* – watch R-rated movies. (Try majoring in the arts; talk about cognitive dissonance!) I have a Canadian friend from the Y who decided which R-rated movies he could and could not watch based on Canadian ratings, which have a rating between PG-13 and R called "M" for "mature." He figured if the movie was "R" in the US but "M" back home, it was okay to watch. (Did I mention that we need things spelled out for us, lest we find loopholes?)

If you are a Mormon, you also know full well that 2-piece swimsuits are of the Devil (as, inevitably, were 1-piece swimsuits when they started to look more like swimwear and less like wet suits). Next time Miss

America comes on TV, (does Miss America still come on TV?!) check out Miss Utah. If she's a Mormon, I can guarantee you she'll be the only contestant in a 1-piece (unless, of course, she wants to damn herself for eternity for all the mortal men she attempted to seduce by showing a six-inch swath of flesh). What about tankinis, you ask? Well, do the two pieces meet? Can you bend over without showing off your tummy? And what about those Brazilian-style "1-piece" suits connected at the sides or in the front and back, with the rest open? Is there the potential for a nearby heterosexual male to spring an erection?

Then you should know better. (Always a qualifier!)

Right about now you're probably wondering why I'm so hung up on all these "little" things about the Mormon experience. What about the positive aspects? How the gospel helps you find deeper meaning in life, make lasting friendships, and learn to serve and love others...

There are great benefits to the Mormon lifestyle, I concede. You have a built-in support network, an attitude of indentured servitude (I mean service), an "eternal perspective" and related set of goals, and an "attitude of gratitude" if you're doin' it right.

We see that attitude of gratitude come flooding out in a giant deluge during every fast and testimony meeting at church. What is fast and testimony meeting, you ask? "Missionary Dread Day." The first Sunday of every month is set aside for "Fast and Testimony" meeting, where everyone in the congregation gives up breakfast and lunch. While small children and pregnant women, etc, etc, are not expected to participate, everyone is expected to set aside the (over-generous amount of) money they would have spent on those two meals to donate as a fast offering. And once everyone has spent the day fasting and is desperate for a single goldfish cracker from the nursery, its testimony time! (It's a bit like Open Mic night at a comedy club, but without the laughter.) Anyone in the general membership who feels "moved by the spirit" is entitled to get up from their seat, wait in a short line for their turn at the pulpit, and then share their testimony with their comrades.

While I believe it was originally intended to inspire a mob-like "I believe!!!" from the congregation, these days it's more like Thankful Day at church. The average testimony on Thankful Day has nothing to do with Jesus or His sacrifice, like missionaries wish it would when they bring potential. Instead, it goes something like this:

"Hi. Um. For those who don't know me, I'm Sister So-and-So…and I just really felt like I had to get up here today so I could publicly tell everyone how grateful I am to have such an amazing (husband/child/family). I had an experience this week where I was just really having a hard time with [insert challenge here], and I prayed about it, and then [insert name here] turned to me randomly on Wednesday night and said [insert nonsense here], and I knew that God was listening and had answered my prayers, and I just feel so blessed and so thankful. I know God answers our prayers, that this Church is True, and we are so blessed to have (a modern day prophet/additional scriptures/Joseph Smith) to guide and direct us in our lives. I say these things in the name of Jesus Christ, Amen."

Sometimes there are tears involved. In fact, you can often tell how hungry the person behind the pulpit is based on how many tears they shed while offering up their Thankfulness. Which leads me to fasting, that great Mormon fallback whenever anyone needs anything – *Let's have a fast!* – that just makes me sick.

No, literally, it makes me ill.

When my husband was a kid (and after he was 8 years old and had been baptized), the kitchen was off limits on Sundays. As a result, he could often be found dry-heaving in the bathroom because his stomach was so upset. My parents never inflicted such torture on us. Most of the time we'd be having breakfast on the first Sunday of the month and someone would say "Aaaw, crap, it's Fast Sunday," and we'd look at each other with these mildly-guilty, mildly-gleeful expressions…and finish our food. "Well, we blew this one! Eat up!"

I can honestly say that I have never *really* fasted a single day in my life (except for a few times I've had the stomach flu, and once for a colonoscopy, but those were by default, and I still had water). My most favorite part (perhaps *only* favorite part) of pregnancy was the excuse not only to *not* fast, but to eat *in* church. Pregnancy aside, I don't fast anyway. Why?

I find fasting sort of twisted.

"Fast. It will bring you closer to God. You'll feel His Spirit more abundantly. It will fill you and cause you to quake and tremble and motivate you to bear your testimony in sacrament meeting. You'll be more visionary as your sacrifice opens heaven's windows for you."

Actually, no. First, I'll be hungry. I might save a couple bucks on food that day, but you'll just want me to turn around and give that cash to you anyway. Second, I won't be closer to God, I'll be bitter that He's into temporary anorexia, bitter with myself for being Mormon, bitter at my "brothers and sisters" with their customary rolls of blubber that keep them from the desperation for sustenance I'm experiencing, and bitter at my non-member friends and neighbors for the heavenly scents wafting through their open windows on my way home from church. Third, I may very well be quaking...from lack of food. Fourth, I may also weep as I bear my testimony (read: tell a story about my rough day/week/year, turning it into a self-aggrandizing anecdote), but it will be due to starvation-induced delirium. Fifth...

Well, I'm actually screwed with "fifth" because the church is correct: I probably will be visionary. Starvation has been known to produce "visions." You, too, would be visionary if you were weepy, shaky, and food-deprived.

And then we participate in the Thankful Day Empathy Party Cry-Alongs, and...sorry, I digress. Back to fasting.

Some people love it. It does something for them, gives them a way to sacrifice their own comfort in hopes that that sacrifice will coax God into bestowing a particular favor or blessing.

I don't fast. Better that I'm fed. (Really, I'm doing us all a favor.) But let them fast, if it somehow makes them feel like they're becoming better people because if it.

Know what else makes us better people? What *else* is beneficial to the lives of...some?

Serving a mission.

Truly, I can't think of anything more awesome for a young man to do with his life at what is naturally the most selfish part of it – 18 to 23-ish – than to devote two years of it to serving and loving the locals in a place completely foreign to him. (I have friends who have served in Central and South America, Asia, the Pacific Islands, Outer Mongolia, Russia, Europe, India, Africa...even as far away as Idaho and Mississippi!) That same young man leaves his parent's home – possibly for the first time in his life! – and lives with strangers in a new place, maybe even speaking a new language, and fending almost entirely for himself when it comes to cooking, shopping, laundry, cleaning, and personal hygiene...which standards are *stringent*. The entire time he is surrounded and enveloped by the people, learning to love them as he believes Christ loves them. Fine, he's trying to convert them, but let's not split hairs: *he's learning to love a group of people outside of his tight-knit Mormon circle.* Most guys his age are either working at hourly grunt jobs for easy pay or pursuing their educational goals for eventual salaried pay. Not this young man. It can be an amazing growth experience. To this day my husband benefits from both the language he learned on his mission and the love he developed for the large ethnic group he served. I'm jealous of his experience, frankly.

But it's not all rosy. Many missionaries head to the Missionary Training Center (MTC), and head right back home. Some get out into the mission field, and *then* head home. (The Miracle of Forgiveness is not only *not* recommended reading for new missionaries, I'm told these days it's *highly discouraged* reading. I believe that book has single-handedly conquered more missionary spirit than any number of sins they may have enjoyed pre-mission!)

A very good friend of mine my freshman year at BYU confided in me that his parents had promised him his choice of any car he wanted once he returned from a successfully-served 2 year mission. He also confided that he had happily handed over his virginity two weeks before to a girl he hardly knew, just in case he got out on his mission and decided it "wasn't for him." He could then confess his sin, and would be rewarded with a one-way ticket back home. (Sometimes a brand new BMW just isn't worth it, I guess.) Another good friend told me that while he'd been on his mission, he'd had sex – twice – with two different girls. I asked him how he'd managed to get away with it, knowing his mission companion was supposed to always be at his side. He said that on at least one of those occasions, his companion was in the next room...having sex with the girl's sister. (You can find tens, maybe hundreds of similar stories online, fyi.)

Then there are people like my very dear friend; we'll call her Melissa. Melissa and I grew up together, and when she hit 21 (because until October of 2012, women weren't allowed to serve missions until age 21) and was not yet married, she decided that perhaps, lacking any other direction, she should serve a mission. Melissa was called to serve in the Philippines. After nine months of eating only rice and fruit, of being bitten by all sorts of foreign bugs and vermin, and of watching the people she was trying to convince of God's love be unable to meet their most basic needs, she fell seriously ill and was sent home, having lost 30 pounds. (My friend is thin; she came home a *waif.*) She wallowed in despair for nearly a year, super-medicated to meet the demands of her crippling depression, and after nursing her back to "health," her parents had no idea what more to do for her, so they sent her to an acupuncturist. In 3 weeks she was no longer depressed, and shortly thereafter decided to pursue a degree in Asian medicine. Much more on her later, jewel that she is, but the reality is that her mission almost killed her.

One more word on the "good" of serving a mission: one of our couple-friends told me that the very best part of her husband having served a mission was that he still had his missionary name tag. Apparently they put it to very, very good use...in the bedroom. In fact, she credits their firstborn child as being a direct result of Daddy's Ongoing Missionary Experience, *a-hem.*

Yeah, that's some naughty sex. But you've got to do something to keep it interesting, frankly. Sex is, from the beginning, taught to youth as "sacred," which means we don't talk about the fact that orgasms feel good. We focus on sperm + egg = gift from God. At some point, though, teens discover that orgasms do indeed feel good...a*nd that's bad.* Sex (until you're married) is naughty, but the moment you're married it's a free-for-all meant to connect you to your spouse and give innocent spirits earthly bodies. Unfortunately, sex was substantially more fun back when it was naughty...which is why our friends have him wearing his missionary name tag in their marital role-playing. *It's naughty.* And it's difficult to make married sex naughty.

But it's impossible to make unmarried sex okay. I should know. I've been through the church disciplinary court(s) to prove it.

There are different levels of "oh-oh" in the LDS church: informal probation, formal probation, disfellowshipment, and excommunication. An example of informal probation would be going in to your bishop to confess feeling up your girlfriend. Your bishop will probably give you something to read – scriptures, The Miracle of Forgiveness, something *light* – and tell you not to take the sacrament for a certain period of time, but (*other than the fact that people occasionally watch to see whether or not you take the sacrament on Sunday,*) no one knows but you and the bishop. If it's more serious, (say you and your girlfriend engaged in oral sex,) he may have to discuss the situation with his counselors, and you may very well be placed on formal probation: you can't take the sacrament for an extended period, you may have extra reading homework, and the bishop will let you know when you're clear, probably after another meeting or two.

Disfellowshipment is reserved either for endowed members of the church (members who have been through the temple, have received their garments, and have made covenants above and beyond the general membership), non-repentant folk who were turned in and have confessed but not repented, or repeat offenders (like me). After you've confessed to the bishop, he meets with his counselors to discuss the situation, and they call you in to ask additional questions, seek clarification about aspects of your sinning, and stare at you with collective hurt and disappointment in their eyes.

By the way, this is referred to in the church as a "court of love." (Feel free to insert your own editorial comment here.)

They send you out of the room so they can come to a verdict on your wickedness, and if you are disfellowshipped, it, like formal probation, shows up on your membership record (only for the length of the continuing issue). During this time you are not allowed a calling, not allowed to pray in church, and not allowed to take the sacrament. People in pertinent organizations are made aware (Relief Society President, Sunday School President, or anyone who would call on you to offer a prayer in church or seek to extend a calling to you), and you then have regular appointments with your bishop to keep him updated on your spiritual progress until he decides you're now a candidate for restoration to full fellowship. At that point, he calls his counselors together again to discuss, they call you in and let you speak your peace (and cry and gnash your teeth and beat your breast; whatever works), send you out like last time so they can confer, and call you back in to either lift or extend your sentence.

It's humiliating, demoralizing, and dehumanizing.

I don't recommend it.

There's excommunication, of course, also reserved for endowed members and non-repentant folk, but very seldom for your basic, unendowed repeat-offender. Usually the sins involved are things that could bring major embarrassment to the church if it retained you as a member, or things that are severe enough that the only way to keep you safe from yourself (instead of letting you eternally damn yourself) is to take you out from under the umbrella of the church. Mormons think of it as a chance to heal without being under covenant not to screw up, like it's a blessing of some sort. While I appreciate that view, and I can see how the leadership might believe it, the meetings are far more in-depth and involve a much wider array of gentlemen, including the Stake Presidency and the High Council members.

I prefer to leave my skeleton closet closed to the Brethren, but *you're* getting a glimpse as I throw these doors open wide to you for just a minute. (Note: If and when my real identity is discovered and Regina's name is discarded, I will be called in for a court of love so that the aforementioned group of stake presidency and high council members – and potentially my current bishop and his counselors – can excommunicate me for being an apostate. Stay tuned.)

So I was disfellowshipped for a time, and then reinstated. (I've been on probation a few other times, to be sure, but never for masturbation, let it be known, because I never confessed to it!) Bottom line: I like sex. I like married sex, I liked sex before I was married…I guess I've always been far too liberated a woman for the Mormon Church.

A roommate of mine was never so naughty. So afraid of naughtiness was she, in fact, that she refused to use tampons because she was afraid it might steal away a portion of her future husband's experience, and was forced (*proudly, head held high*) off her high school swim team because of it. I remember a tearful chat with her two weeks *after* she and her husband married: they had not yet been able to have sex. She was too tight. Seven more days passed before they lost their collective virginity. Eventually she stretched to accommodate, but oh, the pain and embarrassment she might have been spared had she not considered tampons "indecent."

My sweet convert parents have a slightly different idea where "appropriate" is concerned regarding sex and the church. Back in the '70's, when they joined, they felt it important to be married in the temple prior to breeding. (That way they could raise a bunch of B.I.T.CH.es.) They went in for their temple recommend interviews (an interview conducted privately with a member of leadership to determine temple worthiness) with both the bishop and stake president of their area, and on the temple recommend interview back then was the question: "Do you and your spouse engage in oral sex?" Both Mom and Dad, unaware of the answer offered up by the other in their separate interviews, told the bishop "It's none of your business what goes on in our bedroom." In other words, whatever took place in their bedroom was both *consensual* and *private*. Baffled, and with no other reason to exclude them from pursuing the blessings of the temple, the bishop sent them to the stake president, where the scene repeated. Finally the stake president shrugged, signed their temple recommends, and they've been eager temple-attenders ever since.

Imagine, though, how many Mormons in the 1970's were asked to reveal the goings-on in their bedroom…and after they *inevitably openly did so!!!*, were ostensibly prevented from attending the temple if they were honest but not "repentant."

The question disappeared from the temple recommend interview by the time my parents required another interview a year later, but I *had* to ask about it in a Marriage and Family class at BYU. My professor reported that, while it was, at one time, on the list of possible questions a bishop could select as part of the temple recommend interview, the question was now obsolete. The church officially takes no stance and has no comment on the righteousness or unrighteousness of oral sex in the married couple's bedroom.

It still terrifies me that a bishop selected that question.

But I, for one, am relieved by the church's current ambivalence; Mormons everywhere have another naughty loophole!

An additional naughty loophole is the ever-popular sex toy party. If you're not personally familiar with them, they have recently (in the last 10 years) come into vogue, and are Tupperware parties for sex toys. (Mormons love network marketing, so I'm really not surprised, but we'll get to that. All part of being a Mormon.) I have personally held 2 parties, and they are a fabulously fun way of becoming *gently* acquainted with the wonders of modern sex aids, most of which we know nothing about. For Mormons especially, breeding as actively as we do and having all traces of "naughty" disappear from the bedroom the instant we're married, it's important to keep sex interesting. Both parties were well-attended, and one of the two (held in UTAH!) made serious money, selling upwards of $3,000.00 in sex paraphernalia in a single evening.

For the other party, held in California, I emailed a smaller group of people about the event, letting them know that if they were interested, I'd send an invitation, but if not, they should please delete my email and I promised they would hear nothing further from me.

One girl, however, could not resist.

The next morning I received the following email:

Dear Sister Samuelson,

I was concerned when I received your email. I am deeply offended by the idea that you are having a party to make lite (sic) of something me and my husband hold very sacred, which is our wedding vows. I think it is wrong for you to expose other women in the Church to something like this and I am sick for anyone who wants to come. Please reconsitter (sic) doing this. It can only hurt yours and your husband's spirit when you try to be intimate later. The Spirit can't be in the bedroom with people who make lite (sic) of these matters.

With only our spiritual progression in mind,

Sister Self-Righteous

Clearly, I've changed her name.

OKAY, I CONFESS: She stopped me in my reading tracks at "I am sick for anyone who wants to come." All I could think at that point was, "Because clearly you do *not*, Sister!" But I was raised in a convert household, and having been formerly disfellowshipped, I guess I just see sex differently. (Like, *without* the free-floating Spirit of God hovering over my bed watching to see if we are properly sober while my husband and I fuse our souls via our sex organs to create a baby deep within my womb.)

*Tangent warning! During a girls' night out with a dear friend a few years back, I mentioned that what happened in my bedroom was between me and my husband, and we could do whatever we felt comfortable doing. She corrected me: "That's a really horrible way of looking at things, Gina. It's between (sic) you, your husband, and the Spirit of God, and you shouldn't be doing anything that doesn't invite the Spirit to be present when you and your husband are intimate."

That creeped me out, and I told her so...that I couldn't handle the idea of the Spirit present to make certain *his* penis connected with *my* vagina in the *Lord's* fashion. She told me, in turn, that would lead to our participating in degrading things and disappointing God. Dear God: prepare to be disappointed.*

We all see sex differently in this grand Mormon Church...and for the singles, it's got to be pure torture. A friend of my husband's is a single guy, now over 40, which in LDS terms means he is a "menace to society." (Supposed quote from Brigham Young regarding single men over *age 27*, though I have read that the quote may actually be Mormon folklore.) At one point in his post-mission rollicking 20's, he had sex. (Don't act so surprised.) A few years (and a few other "naughty" items not considered naughty by anyone else) later, he was excommunicated. Eventually he was re-baptized, but continues to struggle with his desires.

This sounds more tangential than it is: A couple years ago, my husband and I had the ubiquitous "What would you do if I died?" conversation, and we agreed it would be best that, if one of us passed, the other should shop around for a new spouse and parent for our children. Amazing as each of us are, we knew it would take the other some time to replace us, so I asked what he, specifically, would do if the task of replacing me proved as long and arduous as I'm convinced it would be. (I wish sarcasm translated to print properly.) He replied, "At some point I'd probably just start sleeping around to tide me over until I found the right girl, and we'd just do the temple thing later." I gave him my blessing, primarily because I cannot fathom how anyone – *God included* – could possibly expect a married man who has regular sex to suddenly undergo a dry spell of indeterminate length just because his wife kicks the bucket. After sufficient mourning, I imagine his sex drive would amp back up, and most people will agree that sex is preferable to masturbation. My husband's career is particularly stressful, sex is a great stress reliever, and I believe it *perfectly* reasonable for him to test the waters before jumping into another pool.

As a result, I feel overwhelming sadness for singles and divorcees in the church who have had no success finding a spouse. (Note: widows and widowers NEVER have difficulty finding a new spouse. Once "available" but not "broken" by divorce or "frosted over" from having been a female missionary, widows and widowers are snapped up relentlessly as prime cuts in the LDS Singles Meat Market. Divorcees, not so much.) Imagine having been sexually active at any point – a need, I would argue (though members of the faith would argue instead that, had the individual never taken a bite of the apple, they would not struggle with current cravings) – and then, I don't know…getting divorced. The need remains, but the divorcee is somehow expected to flip a magical hormone switch so they just suddenly don't need sex anymore.

I don't have one of those switches, do you?

Back to my husband's 40-something friend, who at various points during his adult life dared to engage in sexual relations: he is not only not "allowed" to have sex and must feel guilt-laden and sinful for his normal, natural desires, but he struggles with stress, angst, and a general grumpiness that would be so easily relieved by a good two-person orgasmic experience. Furthermore, and here's the kicker for me, when he goes in for a bishop's interview to discuss how difficult it is for him to abstain, the man offering him tidbits of wisdom, strength, and reassurance that he can, indeed, remain celibate then *leaves* the interview, goes home to his family, and has as much sex with his wife as he desires…all while my husband's friend returns home to an empty house and tries not to think about what – or who – he could be doing. He is not a nymphomaniac; he is a normal, healthy human being denied one of our most natural and basic instincts.

Though he isn't a nympho, it's not unusual; I find that there is a *lot* of addiction in the LDS Church. We are addicted to (in no particular order) sex, masturbation, drugs, alcohol, prescription drugs, food (with a vengeance!) and/or sweets, shopping, competition, power, fame, pornography…basically the same things other people struggle with, only we spend so much time telling ourselves we're not allowed to indulge, it becomes all we think about.

Pornography is an excellent example. Most people have accidentally or intentionally viewed some form of pornography at one point or other, and it's a very profitable industry, (particularly if you're Brother Marriott, considering how much money his Marriott hotels make by offering in-room porn movies,) but porn addiction in Utah is notoriously higher than most other states. In fact, in March 2009, Harvard Business School conducted a study on online pornography and discovered that Utahns are the highest per capita online adult entertainment purchasers in the *entire* United States.[ii] Like anything in life used immoderately, pornography can be a very serious addiction, and when utilized by those with an intense belief in its inherent evil, it has a tendency to destroy marriages and families, and create abusive and deviant users. I would argue that if pornography weren't so harped on (and sex weren't so hush-hush), far fewer Mormons would bother, far fewer people would develop addictions, and far fewer families would be torn apart by the other partner's assumption that the addicted spouse has traveled down a path from which they cannot return.

In short, I believe the Mormon combination of *faith* and *culture* breeds *addiction*.

*   *   *

Being a Mormon becomes ever-so-much-more STRANGE when you're preparing to go through the main temple ceremony the first time, known in the church as "taking out" or "receiving" your "endowments." Most of us are encouraged to attend a "temple prep class", where we learn pretty much *nothing*. Then comes the day where you go to the nearest Distribution Center to purchase your very first set of temple clothes, and a few sets of the garments you'll be wearing underneath your clothing for the rest of your life. My mother gave me a temple dress of hers (a long white long-sleeved, high-necked gown modeled on her wedding dress; I loved it!), but she and Dad wanted me to have my own "set" of temple clothing, so Mom and my husband-to-be took me to pick them out. I had not known that one *could* pick out their temple clothes, imagining that there was little-to-no variety inside the temple. (There *is* little-to-no variety; it's more like the half-dozen choices you get with a school uniform.) A woman took the three of us into a back room at the Distribution Center where we could be alone, re-checked my temple recommend (which someone else had checked when I walked in the door), and proceeded to pull half a dozen items out of some drawers. I about hit the floor when, among the myriad bits of white, I spotted bright, screaming green. I remember my future husband trying very hard not to laugh when he saw the look on my face, shocked as I was. (I had expected that everything – EVERYTHING – worn in the temple would be white, as we're required to wear not only a temple dress, but a white slip, white bra, white stockings, white shoes, and white [garments] underclothes. WHITE.) I also needed, it seemed, a white veil, a white six-foot-long swath of pleated white gauzy whiteness, and…a green apron-style square-on-a-ribbon, embroidered with leaves. All I could think was "Adam and Eve" as I stared at it, and it seems I nailed it.

I also had to select garments while at the Distribution Center…without trying them on. I could feel 6 inch square samples of the fabrics, but not knowing anything more about them than how ugly my parents' were, I picked a half-dozen pair in a variety of fabrics and styles, and we walked out of the Distribution Center having spent close to $300. $300, and I was forced to do laundry at least twice a week until we caved and bought me a few more pair.

I had to take those garments to the temple, still in their plastic bags, to prove to the woman preparing me for my endowments that I hadn't actually put them on yet. (That would've been blasphemous.) There they were in their individually-sealed baggies, and I could move on to the Washings and Anointings.

I realize, before I launch into much more, how disappointed some of you may be that I'm not offering a verbatim script of the temple experience, or providing photos of my temple outfit. I see no need to do so when both are readily available all over the internet. Do a search; you won't be disappointed. Instead, I offer the experience to you from the perspective of the young 20-something initiate; very few of the actual details stuck with me, anyway.

Washings and Anointings come first, and you're told to put on your garments. I then collected my temple clothing and was led off to receive my "new name." Everyone who receives their own endowment gets a new name, always Biblical, and always the same for everyone who receives their own endowments on that day. (Considering how few women's names are in the Bible, there aren't many choices, and the only time you ever get a different name from everyone else is when your actual name is the same name they're giving out that day, like Esther isn't given Esther.) The name is supposed to be that which your husband uses at the time of the first resurrection (of righteous saints) to call you up out of the grave. Mind you, my husband received his name when he was 19 and heading out on a mission. To this day I don't know his. He, on the other hand, knows mine, priesthood bearer that he is, and I confess myself a) disappointed when they gave it to me, and b) embarrassed to tell my future husband that when, on resurrection day, he called me forth out of the grasp of death, it would be with one of the ugliest names I've ever heard. I HATED it.

In fact, if I could've walked out then, I just might have.

But you *can't*, you know. Your parents are there, your fiancé is there, everyone is so excited for you and proud of you and, well, if you up and disappeared, the world might end.

On to the next task, then, and this one's major: you file in to the endowment room (me with Mom, who served as my "escort"), and take a seat on, in my case, the left side of the room, where the women sit. (Anyone else in here feel like a Muslim?) On the other side of the room are Dad and my fiancé, both…

OHDEARGOD, are they wearing Chef Boyardee hats?!

Then comes trying desperately not to laugh, and your mom's fingernails digging into your thigh to help you maintain control. *Okay, I think to myself, I have to tell the man I love that he has to call me by a hideous name in Heaven, and that is, indeed, embarrassing, but he's got to wear THAT in Heaven, so I no longer feel quite so bad.*

Eyes back to the front, and we're suddenly receiving piped-in instruction from a booming, disembodied voice explaining that we choose to take these covenants upon ourselves, that if we break these covenants we'll be inciting the Wrath of God, and that if we want to leave now, we only need raise our hands.

I look at my future husband, my father, and my mother in turn, and stay where I am.

Just like every other nice Mormon girl on the left side of the room receiving her own endowments today.

There, but freaked out beyond imagining.

Two hours, much boredom, and lots of signs, tokens, and prayer circles later, and I'm *finally* "passing through the veil" into the Celestial room. I have no idea what I said while I stood in front of that curtain, by the way. It's a big long thing you're supposed to memorize, all while giving secret handshakes to a mystery man through the veil (in this case your future husband, and this is where you tell him your awful new name), and then you're welcomed into a big, beautiful room with a giant chandelier centerpiece and you and your family members can cry and hug and laugh (quietly!) and whisper on some expensive velvet couches for a good five minutes until you're told to move on so the next group can come in.

Now, we were told before we went in that after the endowment was complete, we'd have a chance to ask a temple priesthood authority any questions we had about the ceremony, so I got into the Celestial room thinking "Yay! Now, where's that guy...?" but of course I was immediately mobbed by the aforementioned cry fest. Five minutes later I start looking for this mystery man who will answer all my questions...and we're being ushered out of the room. Was he ever there to begin with, I wondered, or did they just tell us that so they could get us off their backs, or maybe they'll give us those sad puppy dog eyes that say "I'm sorry you missed the secret of life because you were so busy getting a hug from your dad." Either way, I had questions I wanted answered…which sort of baffled me, because there really was nothing about the ceremony, save the funky hand signals and shakes, I thought was anything different from the account of the Creation as laid out in the LDS book of scripture, the Pearl of Great Price. Everyone was always talking about how they learn something new and wonderful every time they go back to the temple, and I came out thinking "What did I miss?"

Frankly, I'm ashamed to reveal how many times I've been back to the temple. If you're Mormon, you'd think it far too few times; if you're not, you'd think I was nuts for having gone so many times. Either way, I'll avoid that Catch-22 and say *I'm done*.

Clearly.

I *can* say that my very *next* temple visit came two weeks later…*at my own wedding*.

My husband is from a very large family; mine is not as large. Even considering the combined size of our respective families, there were exactly eight other people present at our wedding: our parents, one of his siblings and their spouse, and two each of my husband's aunts and uncles. Those were the only available, endowed, worthy members we could scrounge from our families, as some family members were too young to have been through the temple, some were on missions, some were unworthy, and some just couldn't make it.

In particular, one of my sisters was absolutely devastated. She and I have always been close, she was my maid of honor, and yet she sat outside with everyone else (*none* of our other siblings were present during the ceremony) and waited for us to emerge from the temple an hour or two after we'd gone in.

Families may be "forever" in the Mormon Church, but they're not forever until after everybody's dead, apparently.

From what I hear, that experience is fairly typical; it's not until the baby of the family gets married that more of their family members can attend, so the baby gets an odd benefit from bringing up the rear in the marriage department.

But once married – the be-all and end-all for Mormons – what next?

CALLINGS and BREEDING, not necessarily in that order.

The 5th Article of Faith in the LDS Church is as follows: "We believe a man must be called of God, by prophecy, and by the laying on of hands by those who are in authority, to preach the gospel and administer the ordinances thereof." After being handed more than our fair share of major callings at church, with breeding falling somewhere in the mix, and his job acting as a serious drain on our collective sanity, my husband attended the priesthood session of one General Conference. There he heard all about the need to "magnify our callings to the utmost, but still balance family and work and life in general." When he returned home from that particular meeting, my husband announced that the church had changed the 5th Article of Faith. I was all ears. "It is now," he told me, "'We believe a man must be called of God, by prophecy, and by the laying on of *guilt*.'" He didn't bother filling me in on the rest of the meeting.

You see, Mormons *serve*. We serve *all the time*. We serve for free, with "blessings" our only hope of reward.

It used to be, when I was a kid, our church buildings had janitors. NO MORE!

These days the wards who use the buildings have been given the "opportunity to serve" by spending 4 months of each year splitting up Saturdays to volunteer to clean the building: everything from vacuuming, dusting, window washing, pew polishing, and toilet scrubbing, to sweeping and mopping. You name it, we do it. We are now our own janitors, ostensibly to help us better appreciate the buildings (we fund with our tithing money) where we meet and to give us more opportunities to serve, but let's be realistic: janitors receive a salary. Why pay one man for what you can demand for free from hundreds, all based on the promise of invisible and insubstantial "blessings"?

I've been promised "blessings" before, you see, and I didn't handle it well then, either. At one particular point in our marriage we had two very small children, my husband was working obscene hours, was serving as a counselor to the bishop, and I was serving as the Young Women's President. During the Wednesday night youth activities, both my husband and I needed to be present at church, and so my visiting teacher (a die-hard baby fan) volunteered to stay with our children during those 2 – 3 hours every Wednesday night, bless her heart. One evening I returned very late from attempting to comfort a young woman in a difficult family situation, and when I arrived home, noted my husband was not yet home from work/church himself. I ranted for about 30 seconds, angry at the church's drain on our time and emotional resources, until she cut me off.

"You have to remember that the Lord will bless you for all of this. It may seem difficult now, but He wants you to hang in there, to not murmur [grumble], and to know that He loves you and only wants to bless you."

To understand the full depth of my disgust, you'd have to know this woman's situation: she herself had a husband who had worked obscene hours most of his career and served in major callings in the church on top of that, and she has virtually single-handedly raised her 6 children, 5 of whom had either left the church or were in the process of seriously screwing up their own lives. I turned to her, called her by name, and said, "Tell me something. Do you really consider yourself *blessed* for your husband's service? Do you really feel like (insert the names of her children here) have been blessed by not having their dad around? Can you honestly tell me you feel blessed watching your children flounder and never, ever seeing your husband, except on Sundays when he visits the ward and sits halfway across the room on the stand? *Really?*"

I still feel ashamed of my outburst; it was unintentionally cruel, and I probably should have kept it to myself. That said, I was in no frame of mind to handle her challenge just then, and boy, did I take her head off. She went silent, nodded her head a couple times, patted me on the shoulder, and told me she'd see me Sunday. We never spoke about that conversation again, but I stayed the Young Women's President, and she kept coming to play with my kids and, gem that she was, clean my house.

I should've known better. In that ward she and her husband, like my husband and I, were part of what we affectionately referred to as STP: Same Ten People. STP means that there were very, VERY few of us in that ward willing to serve, let alone serve to exhaustion and the brink of insanity. We have since learned that we much prefer being classified as unreliable. In fact, we have made a point of proving thoroughly undependable in every ward we've been in since then so that neither of us will ever receive another marriage-damning call to serve.

Recently the husband of a friend of mine was called to serve on the high council in our stake, meaning he'll never be around on Sundays anymore, and at least a few of his weeknights will be taken up during the month. They have 3 kids, and while obviously slightly overwhelmed, you could also tell how proud they were of her 30-something husband being "promoted" to high priest and given added responsibility in church. My husband and I cringed. Been there, done that, and dear GOD, thank you for preserving our marriage, because we almost didn't make it!

Maybe I'd have survived our calling stints better if I'd had a blessing or two. Blessing, you ask? Yes, blessing. As a Mormon male, you receive the Aaronic priesthood at age 12 or thereabouts, and the Melchizedek priesthood at about 18, or right before you leave for a mission. The Aaronic priesthood allows you to bless the sacrament and perform baptisms (though very few people these days try to baptize anyone unless they've become Melchizedek priesthood holders), and the Melchizedek priesthood (as an Elder in the church) enables you to hold specific callings and give "blessings." (Though there are no additional "priesthoods", there are additional "promotions" that may come, including being made a high priest, a "seventy", an apostle, etc.)

Blessings are of two types: one for comfort, the other for health. Comfort blessings can be offered by any worthy Melchizedek priesthood holder to any blessing seeker; the priesthood holder places their hands on the head of the individual to be blessed, invokes the name of God, and pronounces a blessing on the person in Jesus's name. Dad used to give me and my siblings blessings before we started school each year, and sometimes, if a particularly rough test was coming up (read: the SATs, ACTs, etc.) or one of us was having a hard time socially. It's actually really beautiful when you realize Dad was just telling me the amazing things in his heart, even though they were supposed to be given him of God.

The other type, though, requires at least 2 worthy Melchizedek priesthood holders and involves "consecrated oil", which is extra virgin olive oil blessed by the priesthood holders, sort of like holy water to a Catholic. A drop or two of oil is applied to the scalp of the suffering person, and one of the gentlemen pronounces an anointing blessing, which is to say, you've got sacred EVOO on your head. The second man then joins in and "seals" the anointing, offering the blessing itself.

I've heard blessings promising the individual that they'd be perfectly fine any time now, and blessings telling the person to be stalwart in their suffering because, though the Lord is aware of them, it is not His will that they should be healed "right now," and even blessings releasing people from their mortal lives on earth, kind of like a sort of Mormon "last rights." The majority of the time, however, the blessing is a comfort-*style* blessing advocating patience and assuring the suffering person that everything will happen on the Lord's schedule rather than according to our desire to be healed.

I remember, as a BYU student, thinking "Then why the hell did I bother asking for this blessing? Of course I'll be over this stupid virus soon, and I just need to be patient 'til then. That has nothing to do with *healing me!*"

And yet we seek blessings. A friend of mine who has long-since left the church still asks her father for a blessing every time something rough comes up in her life. Amazing, isn't it, how superstitious a normally very logical person can be?

What also amazes me about being a Mormon is how easy it is to be sucked in to the culture; how you begin to see yourself as righteous – or unrighteous – based on how clearly you fit the mold. I tend to think of Mormon girls as a flock of Alice in Wonderlands: blonde, cute, petite, innocent, wide-eyed and naïve, and more interested in weaving together flower crowns than paying attention to their lessons. After pointing that out to my husband a couple years back, he explained that they weren't so much Alices as they were the Stepford Wives: a bunch of women who, when stripped of their scrapbooks and blogs and crafts and casseroles and babies and hair bleach, lacked both substance and capacity for original thought. One of the first unspoken rules of Mormonism is, after all, obedience. (I suppose it's arguably a *spoken* rule, too.) If you're busy being obedient, there isn't time for original thought, and whether or not we Mormons wish to accept it, very seldom do the obedient and the substantive self have anything to do with one another.

Obedience is key in Mormonism for the obvious reasons, of course – we have a church to keep together! – but within the faith itself, we believe that obedience (to God, His laws, and His modern-day prophets and apostles) brings great blessings and true happiness. What great blessings? That's hardly relevant. If a person is certain that their obedience to the law of tithing is bringing them blessings, it doesn't matter that a tenth of their gross income vanishes into the pocket of a religious organization that never tells us exactly what our money is going toward; we are *blessed.* (Maybe with money, maybe with health, maybe with a stoplight that turns green when we want it to, who knows?) And what is true happiness, according to Mormons? To be reunited with our Heavenly Father in the Celestial Kingdom? Or to have everything go our way here on earth? No one is ever specific.

In fact, the only blessing specifically promised for obedience of any sort (outside of "happiness") is reserved for the *payment of tithing*. Mormons refer to tithing as "fire insurance", having been promised that, so long as we are current with our tithing, we "shall not be burned as stubble at the last day." In other words, be obedient to what the prophet tells you in order to be "happy" and "blessed", and be obedient to the law of tithing so as to avoid incineration.

Quick tangent: one of our couple-friends related the tale of their last ward, where the husband walked in to the clerk's office during church and interrupted four of the brethren comparing their tithing checks with one another, ostensibly to see who wrote the biggest check (and therefore earned the most). It seemed that the conversation had just turned to other members' tithing checks, and they made sport of trying to ascertain the ward's biggest earner. From that day on, our friends opted to send their tithing checks directly to Salt Lake rather than chance that the brethren might see fit to comb through the couple's tithing records, as well. They continued to pay tithing, happy to own stock in eternity and protect themselves against hellfire, but they decided they were most comfortable sending that money straight to church headquarters.

While ten percent of your gross income goes to the church, you may very well be hit up by church members for the other ninety percent: never have I seen a people so obsessed with network marketing. Network marketing, also known as multi-level marketing or "MLMs", offer Mormons get-rich-quick income with remarkably little effort...so long as they get in on it early in the game. With a ward list some four, five, six, seven, or eight hundred people long, Mormons have a built-in group of people to market their overpriced crap to: their fellow church members. For those not familiar with MLMs, they are sometimes referred to by a more recognizable, though markedly less desirable, name: "pyramid schemes." Having personally worked on the corporate end of an MLM, I still find it difficult to express how repugnant network marketing is. People begin to see their friends, family, extended family, and ward "family" as potential – nay, *probable* – customers, alienating most everyone they know in the name of earning a few supplementary dollars off their friends and acquaintances. MLMs sell everything from super-food drinks to body care products to food storage and motor oil, all the way on up to handbags and shoes, home décor and furniture. MLM representatives generally receive their product for a set price and sell it for double their cost, making half the value of the sale. Even as I type this, I can think of at least 20 Mormon women I know personally who are currently involved with an MLM.

None of them are rich. In fact, none of them have made any sort of real living from their MLM.

There are all sorts of ways to get rich quick, supposedly, but when you're a Mormon, you are also supposed to give others a break on the cost of any services you yourself may provide, and go to other members *first* should you require a service *they* can provide.

A ward member needed some furniture refinished, and discovered that a fellow ward member had a hobby of refinishing furniture, so he made a call, agreed upon a price, and handed over a few furniture items. A week later the furniture items were returned, and within days the new finish was flaking in some places, and leaking goo onto his wood floors in other places. The refinisher shrugged when the issue was addressed. "Well," he said, "I'm not a professional. It's just a hobby."

Brother A did a fellow ward member, Brother B, a favor, renting B's home to help prevent foreclosure when Brother B was on the verge of losing his home. Brother A put a considerable amount of his own time and money into the home, and Brother B promised to count $2,000.00 of the ultimate sum as a refundable deposit when the family moved. A few years later Brother A and his family bought their own home, leaving Brother B's house spotless and in excellent condition...better even than when they'd moved in. Brother B then hired another ward member, Brother C, to act as a rental agent, and proceeded to direct Brother C to find considerable fault with the home and accuse Brother A of damage in order to screw him out of the promised $2,000.00. After multiple phone calls and three-way interactions, Brother C shrugged, stating that the rental contract was established before he came on board and this wasn't his problem. Brother B shrugged and told Brother A to prove that he had spent anything on the home in the first place. Brother A and his family moved into their new home, thankfully in a new ward, and are still involved in the legal process to recover their money.

While my husband was working construction in Utah his boss was contracted by a local LDS dentist to remodel the dentist's vacation home in a tiny Utah town. The job proved much more difficult than anyone anticipated, but the dentist approved additional work willy-nilly, and both my husband and the construction crew spent many long hours commuting to and from the home, working from dawn 'til dusk. My husband's boss paid him for his work. The dentist, however, never paid for the work done on his vacation home. He even called the police to come arrest the contractor for "harassing him at work" when he stopped returning the contractor's calls and my husband's boss showed up at the dental office for a chat. Though I imagine the contractor eventually collected his pay, we moved away from Utah before anything was settled…during the course of *two and a half years*.

We recently took a vacation and discovered a friend in our ward was a travel agent. When I began looking into trips and pricing, he confessed that he doesn't normally do business with Mormons; until working with us, he had had few positive experiences with members, many of whom asked him to do considerable footwork and then planned their own vacations, or who expected him to offer them a substantial savings by sacrificing his own livelihood. He is one of an enormous number of Mormons I know – ourselves included – who almost never do business with Mormons. In fact, a ward member contacted me recently to ask me about writing copy for his website, something I do on the side. When I finally quoted him a preposterously reasonable price, he responded with a one line email: "Thanks, I'll get back to you." The following week I found incredibly poorly-written copy on his website, courtesy of a ward member "who wants to learn copywriting" and did it for him free of charge. (He got what he paid for.) Also, I have had a number of people ask me to teach them copywriting, wishing to benefit from my knowledge and experience, my connections and my old copy, but when I mention the price of copywriting lessons, the response is always the same: "Oh, I thought you could just teach me. I mean, I catch on really quick."

Apparently not.

I also know of a self-employed member who works far too hard for his age painting homes and struggling to support his very large family. Two years ago he was asked by a church friend if he would be willing to paint the home of another ward's bishop. He knew of this other bishop, a good man by all accounts, and agreed to give him a free quote. Because the man was a bishop, his quote was substantially lower than the market would bear, but the bishop was unhappy, nonetheless, and talked him down further on the price of his services. He reluctantly agreed because it was a relatively simple job, and thanks to the economy, he was nigh unto desperate for work. A few days into the job, the bishop kept insisting he add new projects and parts of the house...free of charge. The painter *couldn't* say no. (You're thinking, "Sure, he could: no!" But please keep in mind, the client was a *bishop*, which title caries significant weight and implied righteousness. He truly felt he *had* to finish the job.) By the time this poor man had finally completed the project, he had *lost* money. The bishop refused to pay any more than the originally agreed-upon price, leaving the painter discouraged, out a considerable sum, sore from many days' back-breaking labor, and heartbroken when he had to explain the situation to his wife.

But in the Mormon Church, we serve each other (free of charge!) *all* the time. Take our last bishop, a realtor who worked eighty hour weeks anyway, then served as bishop (often a forty hour per week job) free of charge. He was expected to lead a ward 400 people strong, mediate issues betwixt multiple parties in the ward, listen to confessions, plan and execute Sunday services and weekly activities, participate in scores of weekly meetings, be familiar with each individual in the ward and all their myriad struggles, ensure that his ward members had sufficient food, clothing, and housing, help them locate jobs if they were out of work, and be a spiritual and emotional pillar of strength, as well as an example to everyone around him...*all the time.* We became good friends with Bishop and his family, and my husband is personally familiar with the struggle that was that calling. I remember explaining with pride to a non-member friend that our leaders were all lay people who had other jobs on top of their callings. As much as we love Bishop and his family, however, until I stepped away from the church and looked at it from an outsider's perspective, I had not seen the foremost glaring issue with Bishop as a bishop: here was a real estate agent offering the services of a trained counselor 24 hours a day, 7 days a week...without any training. Other than 4 years in high school seminary (he never attended BYU), he had no formal ministry training and no training in how to cope with what he would inevitably encounter, listening to the woes and confessions of 400 people. My pride in a lay clergy instantly evaporated, but my horror at having confessed items of a personal nature to a BYU professor, an accountant, an insurance salesman, an electrical subcontractor, and a shipyard manager (all various bishops of mine) increased exponentially.

I had also spent many years defending the church-paid income of the general authorities, noting that when you're an apostle traveling around the country – and the world! – to preach of Christ's church, you don't have the time to work another job. (As though Bishop's 120-hour workweek left him time enough even to sleep!) I didn't realize all those years that each of those apostles may very well be "earning" a *six-figure income* while the lay clergy busts their butts doing church jobs (for which they are seldom qualified) for free on top of their day jobs. (Note: that sum was suggested by an anonymous former Church Office Building employee to Kay Burningham, author of <u>An American Fraud: One Lawyer's Case Against Mormonism</u>, and is reported in her book, though the number cannot be confirmed.)

I personally defended these men. After all, they are priesthood holders, and where the prophet and apostles are concerned, they are eligible to receive direct revelation for me as a member of their church. They're like Mormon rock stars, really. I remember, as a BYU student, attending a devotional with about 30,000 other students where President Gordon Hinckley spoke, and the excitement at the Marriott Center was palpable. When Hinckley finally arrived, we all leapt from our seats, spontaneously broke into the hymn, "We Thank Thee, O God, for a Prophet," and two of the half-dozen freshman friends with me actually wept. When Hinckley finished and made his way back out of the building, he paused a few times to wave to every quadrant of the building, and I absolutely felt like he was waving personally to me. Until now, I've never related hearing from the prophet to being present at the Ed Sullivan show for a Beatles performance, but that's exactly what it was like. These men are practically GODS.

Every word they speak becomes doctrine (so long as it is spoken across the pulpit in the Conference Center in Salt Lake City during one of the twice-yearly General Conferences), and is directly from God for our ears...but *only* that of the priesthood holders. I recently confessed to my husband the combination of horror and submission I endured in our early marriage as we watched Conference one Sunday, and he was duly repentant, bless his heart. One of the speakers, an apostle, concluded his talk, and it was time to hear from the General Relief Society President, a woman. My husband immediately stood and headed toward the kitchen, eager for a snack. "Where are you going?" I called after him, baffled. He had watched the apostle speak with rapt attention, but seemed to have suddenly given up on Conference.

"I'm hungry," he explained, sticking his head through the doorway. "Besides, she's not a priesthood holder. She won't have anything but some sappy stories to tell; it's not like she can receive revelation for the entire Church or anything."

I was at once struck by how unfair that was, being a woman myself and thereby being accused of having nothing to offer because by default I lacked priesthood authority. I was also disgusted with myself for having ever believed that women, who don't have the priesthood, had anything legitimate to offer during Conference. Because this troubles me so much to this day, I must rephrase and repeat: His comments jarred me. I was angered by the idea that my husband believed women had nothing to offer the general membership, but at the same time appalled at myself for having thought a woman could communicate anything worthwhile to the church *because they could not, without holding the priesthood, receive revelation for the entire church directly from God.*

As a woman I was worthless to my faith (outside of the warm fuzzies produced by my standard drivel).

Please note that until about six months ago, NONE OF THIS OCCURRED TO ME AS WRONG.

Until my husband had a chance to peruse this manuscript, he himself had not thought anything of it. Please note: he has apologized profusely, and I have happily accepted his apology, knowing full well that he, too, had been just as indoctrinated.

That's what it's like to be a Mormon.

In the same vein, there are officially six sessions of conference: the General Women's Conference, which takes place a week or two before "real" Conference, usually a feel-good meeting attended entirely by devout women. The remaining five sessions are held over a weekend, twice a year in April and October: two sessions (morning and afternoon) on Saturday, two on Sunday, and one Saturday night called Priesthood Session, attended only by men. The express purpose of this meeting is to lead and guide the men in their church and familial duties, and to impart to the men any new "revelations", which are then to be disseminated to their families upon their return home. In other words, God gives revelation to the prophet, the prophet gives revelation to priesthood holders, and priesthood holders pass on revelation to their women and children. It wasn't until recently it ever occurred to me to wonder how the single women in the church ever got to hear the "good stuff"…or to see clearly *exactly* how devalued we women are.

I, for one, have never felt particularly valued by the Mormon Church. I tend to stand out from the crowd a bit, having been an arts education major and having a wild creative streak as I do, though I admit that drawing attention to myself (contrary to popular belief) has never been my intention. I have just always wanted to like what I like, do what I do, and be who I am without feeling like the "real" me is an inappropriate person to be. I value my uniqueness, but I have found, as a Mormon, my uniqueness is alternately hated and over-appreciated. I constantly receive eye-rolls from my fellow members. "Oh, that's just Sister Samuelson. She's a little *different*." Additionally, as one content to emphasize my best physical features via makeup and wardrobe for church on Sundays, ("Sunday best," right?) sometimes those very same eye-rolls are accompanied by erections, at least where men are concerned. They may be too intimidated to speak to me, but they're *not* too intimidated to further devalue me by thinking of me as a sex object…even a modestly-dressed one.

Damned if you do, damned if you don't.

In my last few wards I have experienced rampant judgment. I realize this is not the case in all wards – we have lived in wards where my individuality was a source of joy rather than amusement, and I loved those wards – but my most recent experiences have been primarily negative. Judgment comes from all sides, but is worst amongst the women; I often feel like I'm watching a "Church Lady" sketch on Saturday Night Live when I hear them gab.

Most recently, they've been offended by my unfriending them on facebook. (Note: I sometimes think facebook is the bane of my existence. You can't ever leave any part of your life behind anymore, and considering how different I am today from the person I was 20 or 10 or even 1 year ago, there are just some people I don't want to be forced to reconnect with.) Hurtful comments abound, (thank GOD I don't have to read them!) but I've been run through the ringer before by those same petty high school-minded women (who, like the Church Lady, absolutely believe it is their "right" and "duty" to assess a stranger's motives and judge their behavior), and I confess I'm relieved to be rid of those "family" members.

The most difficult part of being judged by your "family" is that because we are not *actually* family, no one outside my spouse has any clue what is really going on in my head, or what our circumstances entail...nor do they care. It is enough that they know I am not a Stepford Wife; everything else is, therefore, fair game.

In order to fit in with the Stepfords, you can be motivated to do things you might not normally do. Seeking acceptance can also convince you that behaviors or actions you know are unacceptable are just fine because someone else is Mormon, and they're doing it. I cannot possibly describe how horrified I was teaching in a Utah school: though 95% of each class was LDS, *just like in other schools around the country* 50% of the kids were doing things they should not have been doing, which meant that nearly 100% of the kids participating in illicit activities were LDS. It's rather like dominoes; once one tries ecstasy, and he's Mormon, suddenly lots of kids are using E because the first kid (and those that followed him off the cliff) tried it. I'm not just talking high school kids justifying their actions, either; I'm talking junior high, elementary, college...and adults. People who actually *believe* that drinking coffee is wrong but *do it anyway* because a few of the other Mormons at work do, too. They feel justified committing "sins" because their fellow members are committing those same "sins," meaning that either a) they don't really, deep down, believe what they're doing is sinful, or b) if other people are doing it, it's not so serious that they, too, can't get away with it.

Living life that way is agony. For those of us that try to be true to ourselves, it's just as difficult, thanks to the aforementioned judgment. Many months ago one of my children sought the opportunity to participate in Testimony Meeting by bearing their testimony. Dad was away on business, so Mom was left to provide an escort to and from the podium. This presented a major problem for me: almost every parent who is forced to walk their child up to the stand so they can babble for a minute in the microphone must themselves turn to the microphone and bear their testimony, as well. But even then, I wasn't sure I had one. (Note: I was the GOSPEL DOCTRINE TEACHER at the time.) There I was, up in front of probably 500 people that day, trying to follow up my child whose testimony was as follows:

"I know this church is true, I'm thankful for my family, and I say these things in the name of Jesus Christ, Amen."

My kid gets off easy, in other words, and there I am, all eyes on me. So what do I tell them? The truth: I don't "know" this church is true. I don't "know" Jesus lived, that Joseph Smith was a prophet, or that Thomas S. Monson is our modern-day prophet...but I *hope*. I hope that that's all true, and I hope that the Lord will welcome me back home after I die and stand before me at the bar of God and offer Himself and His sacrifice in my behalf. (I closed as usual.)

You could've heard a pin drop. I actually saw a couple people nod as I spoke – I think they got me – but the firestorm I created was nothing short of torture. The moment I left the podium three people came forward to wait their turn in line, and after the next guy – we'll get to him – five more followed. A couple kids jumped up after those eight, and by then the meeting had gone way over. But it was the speaker who went right after me who really got the ball rolling.

Yes, he got right up to that microphone and pointed – POINTED – down at me, sitting there all alone with my kids. He said something to the effect of "I've been there, too" but then proceeded to correct me. "Sister Samuelson, I want you to stop and think about what you've said. You *do* know the church is true. You *do* know that Joseph Smith was a prophet and that Jesus died for you. We've all heard your lessons. You may not know you know, but I promise you, deep down *you do know*."

The following speaker's testimony was short: "Sister Samuelson may not feel like she knows, but I can testify to all of you that *I* know. I know that [fill in the blank with the usual drivel], and that [add a little more]. This *is* the true church, the gospel of the Lord Jesus Christ..." (Yadayadayada.)

The third speaker addressed me personally again. There's no point relaying her comments; she said pretty much the same thing as the first two combined. By the end of sacrament meeting, however, six of the eight testimony bearers had either addressed or referred to me personally, most of them correcting me with a "Yes, you do!" My favorite bit, though, was the look on my bishop's face when he stared down upon me from his place on the stand, all at once pitying and patronizing.

So much for being true to myself.

66

Instead I'm hounded to be more like others, and so is my husband. After two solid months of missing church thanks to his job in this global economy (where church falls during the Monday morning working hours of one of my husband's offices) and constant 100-hour workweeks, my husband made a point of attending sacrament meeting one Sunday, knowing he would have to bug out the moment the 75 minute meeting concluded. As the prayer ended with an echoing "amen," one of the ward leaders leapt from his chair and made a beeline for my husband. There was no "Where have you been? We've missed you," no "Anything we can do for your family?" not even a "How are you, Brother Samuelson?" No, the first thing out of this gentleman's mouth was "So, Brother, we have a goal amongst the Brethren in the ward to get 100% on our home teaching, and right now you're the only one dragging down our numbers. What do we need to do to help you get your home teaching done so we can reach our 100% goal?"

As though my husband didn't have enough to worry about, and wasn't already wondering if anyone had even thought of him these last two months, let alone missed him. Turns out he didn't have to worry; he had been greatly missed. (Or at least, his home teaching efforts had.) You see, each of the men in the ward is assigned a certain number of families that they are supposed to "home-teach." That means once a month they meet with each of those families in that family's home and deliver the same two-page "lesson" from the general authorities that the father in that family presumably already shared with the families *they* home teach, but that's irrelevant. Point is, each family is visited, and any problems, concerns, and woes they may wish (or be coerced) to share are then reported back to the ward by the home teacher. The women do the same – visiting teaching – but it's just women with other adult women, not woman to family. (Yes, women must therefore sit through two visits while their husband and children sit through just the home-teaching visit.) Mind you, my husband was already working over 100 hours each week to support his family; his home teaching assignment (always assigned, never declined!) was just about the very last item on his priority list. He did not take kindly to this man's passive-aggressive rebuke and went – not back home, but to work! – far more frustrated and depressed than uplifted and spiritually prepared for another 100-hour workweek.

I had a similar experience while living in Utah. My visiting teaching supervisor – a woman I did not know and couldn't ever remember having met – called one evening out of the blue to ask if I'd completed my visiting teaching. I told her I hadn't. She then asked me this question (and I can quote it verbatim, it was such a slap across the face): "So…are you ever actually going to *do* your visiting teaching, or should I just call your companion and make sure she's doing it?" (Many times home and visiting teachers are assigned a companion to accompany them on visits, but not always. Honestly, at that point I didn't even know I *had* a companion.)

I was shocked. I think I told her that she'd need to get my companion to do it, she replied with a "fine," and disconnected the call (read: hung up on me). I cried on and off for an hour until my husband got home, saw my tear-streaked face, and pried the story out of me. He then leapt on his big white horse, called the Relief Society President and informed her of the conversation that took place between me and my supervisor, then demanded that I be released from my visiting teaching assignment, as I was not in a position (spiritually/mentally/ physically) at the time to be out forcing my friendship onto women I did not know. That's really what visiting teachers are, after all: assigned friend-spies.

It's like being a member of the Nazi party! Seriously! BYU was the worst, and again, I'll get to that, but that's really what's expected of the membership: keep an eye on everyone, and inform the Relief Society President and/or the Bishop *immediately* if someone to whom you're assigned has a need or a spiritual deficiency "so that the Church can help."

I received some of that trickle-down "help" when I was serving in Young Women's a few years back. I was incredibly pregnant – I had only a month left to go – and had no skirts or dresses that would accommodate the giant torpedo out in front, and certainly wasn't going to buy one just so I could wear it for four Sundays. So, with the bishop's express permission (which I intentionally sought because I wasn't up to catching flak), I wore very attractive loose, flowing black pants to church. I remember Bishop's response when I asked him, by the way: "I don't give a rip what you wear to church. Show up in pajamas, for all I care; just show up!" Bless him for that.

But not everyone felt similarly. The Young Women's President at the time was apparently horrified at the example I was setting for the young women. Her first counselor usually provided my in-class presidency member oversight, but since her counselor had been home sick that day, it fell to the president to take note of my attire. She passed on word of my wearing *pants* to church to her counselor the next day, and that Wednesday the counselor and I – very good friends and constant sushi buddies – went out for a girlfriends' sushi dinner. I recall the conversation all too well:

"So," she started, "can I ask you something without your getting offended?"

I wrinkled my brow. "You know you can."

"Because Sister YW President told me something the other day, and I could hardly believe it." I waited. Nothing.

"Okay?" I prodded her.

"Did you really wear *pants* to church last Sunday?"

I motioned – with both hands – to my ridiculously large belly. (Yes, we ate sushi, and no, my child suffered no brain defects.) "Have you seen this thing hangin' off my front?"

"Yeah, but...*pants*?"

I laughed. For a while. "First and foremost, I don't fit into my churchy maternity clothes. Second, they were tactful black pants, and they happen to look like a long swishy skirt when I waddle, which is what I do these days. Third, and most importantly, I cleared it with Bishop."

"You did?!" She was honestly, truly in shock. "What did he say?"

"He told me to wear pajamas if I wanted, so long as I showed up."

That settled it, and not another word was said...until she showed up at my house two days later with half a dozen maternity skirts and dresses.

Needless to say, I *continued* to wear pants for the final three weeks of church until I popped, trying not to grin gleefully at the Young Women's President each time I wore them, and I returned my friend's clothing shortly thereafter.

Another instance of "help" came more recently. My Relief Society president, who is exactly my age but has twice as many kids, came by to see me, worried because I haven't been to church much lately and because I had asked to be un-assigned as a visiting teacher. We talked for a few minutes and I told her, quite candidly, that I had never received a confirmation that the Book of Mormon was "true." She offered her very best advice: "Sister Samuelson, I know you're a very logical, intellectual-type person. Your lessons were always wonderful and showed that you really put a lot of thought and research into them. That said, sometimes you really just have to try not to THINK."

No, seriously. She said that. To me. But I digress:

"…try not to THINK. Some things just require faith. If you think too much about it, you might end up walking away, and I would hate to see that happen."

"But Sister Relief Society President, I really have tried the faith bit…so how long am I supposed to wait for an answer?"

"As long as it takes."

"Yes, but that's assuming it's true."

"It IS true," she assured me. "And while some people are blessed with a strong testimony, some of us are blessed with the ability to rely on other people's testimonies. Maybe you're just one of those people."

What could I say to that? It's really hard to argue a point to a woman who is currently advocating that you should STOP all that AWFUL THINKING. (I could go on about this for the next three days, but the truth of the matter is that her heart is in the right place…even if her logical mind is somewhere else.)

I had actually attempted to make use of her "logic" once before: when I was 13 I babysat regularly for a wonderful young Mormon family with two small kids. Not having received an answer to my BoM query, I mentioned to the couple upon their return home one night that I was struggling. They sat down with me there in their living room, and Brother 30-Something proceeded to share with me a very personal experience he had had that had confirmed to him the truth of the LDS faith: he had seen Jesus. I won't go into any details, but I relied on his testimony for fully two years before I tried again at 15 to discover for myself the legitimacy of the Book of Mormon.

It's not that I doubt his claim, but throughout history people have seen, heard, and felt any number of gods – myself included – and I still haven't the foggiest idea if any of it is legit, or just our hopeful minds playing tricks.

Anyway, I am NOT blessed with the ability to rely on the testimonies of others. Sorry, Sister Relief Society President.

I promise to move on to some of the reasons I have decided against belief in the LDS faith in a few pages, but there are two more wholly-unrelated items about what it's like to be a Mormon that I simply must address: Mormon Spin, and Mormons as parents. Please bear with me just a little longer; I might entertain you!

Mormon Spin is interesting, and something you've probably already picked up on: we see what we want to see. If all the stoplights are green between here and WalMart, we've clearly earned some amazing blessings in this life; we just have to learn to see them. If all the lights are red between here and Café Rio, it's not that we've been cursed. It's that God knows someone will run a red light a mile or two ahead, and if we are in that place at precisely that moment, we might be killed. Those red lights were God protecting us, even though, thanks to our impatience, we might not really have deserved it. And when a baby – *my* baby – is in my arms during a walk-through of a newly-built temple that has yet to be dedicated and reaches, giggling, for a giant sparkly chandelier overhead, it is *clearly* because there are spirits there with us in the room floating overhead, delighted by the temple's having been built for the sake of their redemption. It just so happens that my six month-old is the only one who can see them. How cute.

I suppose all religions utilize Spin. In fact, technically I covered it when I mentioned blessings, but the degree to which is it utilized by Mormons has *got* to exceed that of at least *some* other faiths. We read God into everything, good and bad, big and small. Out of Froot Loops? God didn't want you eating sugary cereal that day; don't blame your brother. Bombed the big test you studied for all week long? God has other plans, not to worry. Your bonus was bigger this year than last? God blessed you for striving to support your family. (Be sure to pay your tithing!) In the LDS faith there's no room for coincidence, no space for the natural order of things, and to come back to it, no possible chance that God *won't* answer your prayer. He'll just do it when He's darn good and ready, and He'll answer it in His own way. (Aah, cognitive dissonance.)

On to Mormon Parenting. Perhaps I didn't it notice when I was young, or perhaps things have changed as my generation has become the 20- and 30-somethings of today, but Mormons parents tend to be atrocious. They are permissive, buddy-like, and have no backbone, letting their kids do as they please and expecting nothing of them but that they "enjoy their childhood." (I often wonder if that's because of the burden of responsibility borne by LDS adults who want their kids to be kids as long as possible before taking on churchly duties.) Maybe this generation of LDS parents is just following society's lead, or maybe it's something deeper. I honestly don't know. What I do know is that when I sit down in sacrament meeting, I expect to be able to hear the speaker. The occasional squeak and squeal, I understand; children screaming NO!NO!NO! at the top of their lungs, I do not. (Even though I feel their pain.) I expect that people's children will remain in their seats for the majority of the meeting. Squirmy and bored I understand; jumping up and down on pews and running up and down aisles, I do not. I expect that children will be encouraged to entertain themselves with some sort of quiet activity during the meeting. Drawing, origami, coloring, reading, or, where teens are concerned, even texting I understand; banging on chairs, consuming (and dumping on the floor) vast amounts of snacks, and throwing tantrums...

In all honesty, I've never brought anyone, Mormon or otherwise, to our current ward that wasn't *absolutely appalled* by the behavior of the children there.

From the time our children were little, we came prepared: we supplied them with crayons and coloring books, board books, paper and pencil, origami sheets, even tiny toy cars to roll over the hymn books. We brought little treats as incentives – a single Jolly Rancher lasts a really long time! – and taught them tic-tac-toe and hangman, and the American Sign Language alphabet to deliver their guesses. There were occasions, particularly when our kids were very small, that they just couldn't stand a 75 – 90 minute meeting. Naptimes were missed, lunchtimes were missed, and sometimes kids are just grumpy. Those instances offered us a special opportunity to teach our children that sitting in sacrament coloring and sucking on hard candy was far preferable to a variety of miserable alternatives. Even serving in the bishopric, my husband was there to help our children experience those alternatives. Sometimes that meant sitting on Dad's lap in a dark and silent classroom doing nothing at all. Sometimes that meant sitting in a hot car with Dad, all buckled in but not going anywhere. Regardless of the alternative presented, each of our children decided very quickly that sitting quietly in sacrament rolling a toy car up the spine of a hymnal wasn't so bad after all.

It's a simple thing to teach, but it takes consistency, perseverance, and sometimes self-sacrifice. (I assure you, Daddy suffered *far more* sitting in the hot car dressed in a full suit than either child ever did.) Once taught, however, the lesson is learned, and it generally need not be taught again.

Still children run wild through the chapel on Sunday, steam-rolling other kids and reeking general havoc on the ward, and their parents do nothing.

By way of extreme example, a few years back during a Father-Son Campout one of the men in the ward pointed out the behavior of second man's son: the boy was chasing down children half his age (and size) with a Nerf baseball bat, beating the bloody piss out of all of them. The father's response? "Eh. Those kids just need to man up."

Three and four year-old children need to *man up*?

Really?

I cannot begin to express my relief that my husband and son missed that particular outing. Had my husband been present, he'd probably have beat the living hell out of that father, telling *him* to "man up," and my sweet husband would still be serving jail time.

It's not that Mormon parents are – or should be – any better parents than anyone else. If I'm being honest, it's that I expect more from them. They profess to live to a higher standard than others because they "know better". They profess to know the Truth, to know God and His Son Jesus Christ, to know the Gospel in its entirety, and yet time and again, and most especially where their children are concerned, they just… don't…get it.

Or maybe they don't care.

Or maybe they're too self-involved.

Maybe they weren't taught properly.

I truly do not know…but I expect more. Maybe that's *my* problem. Nonetheless, there's no more terrible feeling than sending your sweet, innocent, well-behaved children to their *church class* knowing that the behaviors to which they will be exposed are far worse than those of their *public school* classmates. It's infuriating!

Infuriating, sad, exhausting: those are three PHENOMENAL words to describe what it's like to be Mormon. As a Mormon I found myself almost always depressed. Now that I've finally accepted my disbelief, I cannot express my joy. I cannot express my relief.

For the first time ever – ***EVER!*** – I finally feel *free*.

The Historical Church

If we're going to begin, it should be at the beginning. In my case, my doubts have always gone further than just the Book of Mormon. The idea that a donkey had a chat with someone, or that God turned a woman to salt to punish her curiosity but then okayed her drunk husband sleeping with his own daughters, or pretty much *anything* to do with the Noah story – and thousands of other tales – have bothered me since childhood. I may have a strong imagination, but even I am generally able to differentiate between fact and fiction.

Samson murdered a thousand men with an ass jawbone over what amounts to an insult, and God sanctioned it? I struggle with that. Add on the Book of Mormon, with no solid proof that it's anything but bull poo, and throw in the Doctrine & Covenants, where I realized very early that Joseph Smith could say anything he wanted "in the name of the Lord." Include the Pearl of Great Price, "translated" from papyri by Joseph Smith that just happened to wind up in his lap (for $2,400.00) though it was supposed to have been written thousands of years earlier by Abraham himself (we'll get to that). While other members were saying, "YES, and thanks be to Heavenly Father for making it all possible!" I was scratching a head full of cognitive dissonance and saying, "Wait, what?"

I realized at that point that it was all or nothing. The LDS faith taught me that Mormonism and Catholicism were my *only* two choices in a Christian religion – restored, or never lost – and I had also been taught all the reasons why the Catholic Church was the biblical Whore of Babylon. If ever I discovered that the LDS faith was so much horseshit, there could be nothing else. Worse, debunk the Book of Mormon, the D&C, the Pearl of Great Price, or even one single thing Joseph Smith preached – *any* one of them – and Joseph Smith was not a prophet, which left the Catholics, who were wrong, which left…

Absolutely no Christian faith whatsoever.

When you step back and really get a sense of just how big the forest is, sometimes it's easier to disappear back into the trees.

At some point, though, we mature enough to face our demons, and in my case, the demon I came face to face with was none other than Joseph Smith. Very few historical characters interest me as he does, because in *all the wrong ways*, I feel like I can relate to him.

That's not a comfortable confession to make.

As I've grown, I've seen this religious leader (spoken of in hushed voices and testified to – by people who never knew him – as a prophet) spill his secrets. The skeletons in our respective closets are similar. He is an imaginative, engaging, self-aggrandizing compulsive liar, and so am I.

Did I actually just type that? YIKES! But I'm being entirely honest here: courtesy of "lying for the Lord" and the aforementioned cognitive dissonance, I think it's safe to say that the church has bred within me a propensity for devising "spiritual" lies. God help me!

Had I been left unchecked and lived as a man in the 1800's, I'm fairly certain I'd have BEEN Joseph Smith. However disconcerting that may be for me, it is the truth. Thankfully, noting those traits in myself at various points in my life, I have done my utmost to channel my imagination into positive action, and been able to tackle the other negative attributes so that I'm on the proverbial wagon. But I was not always, and am not always, and those times made and continue to make it easy to see Joseph Smith looking back at me in the mirror.

What sort of a man was Joseph Smith? As the founder of Mormonism and a simple, charming trickster from the northeast US, it takes a great study of history, legal documents, and journals to piece him together. He is quoted as having said "No man knows my history. I cannot tell it; I shall never undertake it." Instead, Fawn Brodie undertook it in her seminal work, No Man Knows My History. Should you wish to know all the ins and outs of Joseph Smith, I strongly suggest you read her book. (For an opposing viewpoint, read Rough Stone Rolling, by Richard Lyman Bushman.) I will not bother going into any grand detail regarding what Brodie has covered so beautifully. Instead, I offer you (in brief) the juxtaposition of what I was raised to believe about Smith versus what Brodie has to say, and why I no longer believe what I was taught. (Again, if you're interested in a full-scale spread of all the facts about Smith's life, read Brodie or Bushman. If I spelled it all out for you here, this book would cease to be a confessional and become a historical work, which is not my point.)

In the church we are taught that a 14 year-old Joseph, unable to choose betwixt Christian sects, knelt in a grove of trees to ask God which church He wanted Joseph to join. God and Jesus appeared to him, told him to join none of them – that they were all a bunch of malarkey, which assertion delights Christians to this day, you can imagine, sarcasm, sarcasm – and assured him that he had a mission to restore the truth to the world, and that they'd get back to him.

Clearly I'm paraphrasing, and will be throughout this whole section. Again, if you want specifics, please refer to Brodie and/or Bushman!

After much prayer and devotion he was finally allowed to glimpse the golden plates, having been directed to them by an angel, but he was not allowed to touch them. A few more years passed and God handed them over, Joseph translated them, and VOILA! we have the Book of Mormon and the beginning of Mormonism.

Except according to a large number of conflicting records, that's not what happened.

The account of the "first vision" was actually a hodgepodge of four accounts, the canonized version drafted last, and his supposed age at the time of the vision ranged from 14 to 21. The accounts are all vastly different, as well; sometimes he saw one or more angels, sometimes God, sometimes Jesus, who was God, and eventually God and Jesus, as he had apparently decided by the time of the last draft that they were two separate people. His official version, included in our scriptures, was written decades after the vision was supposed to have occurred.

This *isn't* what we're taught in Sunday school, nor is it disclosed to possible converts, which group of people Mormons refer to as "investigators". (I guess it isn't "uplifting" enough.)

Editorial comment warning! Hard to "investigate" something fully when you're only given a small part of the evidence, isn't it?

Joseph allegedly experienced his first vision in 1820, when God told him not to join any church because none were "true."

Eight years later he joined the Methodist church! I hadn't been taught that, either, but you can see my conundrum upon learning that such was the case.

I mentioned earlier that I believe Joseph Smith was a compulsive liar. I also believe that he used his imagination and his engaging personality to convince people he *wasn't* full of crap. In fact, in

Burningham's book, she quotes a drunken Joseph Smith as having said, in reference to his followers, something to the effect that he'd "never met a bigger bunch of dupes." He lied about everything, all the time, weaving a tangled web so insanely full of falsehood that I honestly feel there were moments when he *actually believed it all himself.* (I've been there, sad to say.) He lied until his very death when, at the last moment, he yelled "Oh Lord, my God…" as he fell from a window – not a spiritual reference, by the way, but a special plea to his Masonic brethren for help – and then crawled to a nearby well where he died, full of lead balls from the guns of some very pissed off mob members.

We are taught, by the way, that he was shot while standing by the window and fell out of it. We are NOT taught that he had a weapon, that he fired into the hallway and killed two men (in self-defense, yes, but not something I could imagine Ghandi doing), that he hit the ground still alive, that he crawled to a well and begged for his life, or that a bunch of men unloaded their weapons into his body. We are also not taught that the "mob" came after him because he had propositioned the wife of one William Law, who then lambasted Smith in the only issue of the Nauvoo Expositor ever printed, (Law's new paper,) and Smith ordered (against the 1st amendment!) the printing press destroyed. Smith had gotten off scott-free in a number of other court cases, and those men wanted western-style justice.

I've heard people argue repeatedly that Joseph would never have been willing to die for something that wasn't true.

Bull crap.

As an always-recovering compulsive liar (again, courtesy of lying for the Lord and cognitive dissonance – thanks, Mormonism!), I can *personally* attest to it being bull crap.

First of all, he *wasn't* willing to die, hence his plea to the Masons. Forgive me, but that cry out the window was a serious "oh, shit!" moment. Second, THE MAN HAD TWO GUNS IN THE ROOM WITH HIM. (Oh, how I WISH I was making this up!) And third…actually, allow me to illustrate my point before I make it.

When I was in 4th grade, I had a kind and loving teacher. Two years later, in 6th grade, I was in the girls' bathroom with a couple other friends, and we, like so many 11 year-olds, decided to try our hand at spit wads. We each grabbed a small handful of toilet paper, soaked it in running water, squeezed out just a bit of the water until the toilet paper was squishy, and chucked those things at the ceiling, delighted when they stuck. Being both brave and stupid, I went first. My two friends followed one by one, and as the latter's wad left her hand, a 4th grader walked into the bathroom, saw what was happening, and ran to tell her teacher...which teacher had been ours two years before. She showed up in no time, and the three of us were taken to an alcove and offered a chance to explain.

I lied through my teeth, claiming that the girl who had *actually* thrown the final spit wad was a 5th grader wearing almost exactly the same outfit as my friend, and she had run out of the bathroom only moments before. I insisted that, should our former teacher make the attempt, she'd easily locate the real offender on the playground. I also explained that the girl had thrown *three* spit wads, and was entirely to blame for the mess on the ceiling. The teacher questioned us further, but I was the only one who spoke; the other two did not correct me. I continued to insist that my friend was innocent, finally stating that we felt so terrible for not having been able to stop the real criminal from running away, we would be happy to help the janitor tidy up the bathroom.

My old teacher stared me down. I stared right back, unflinching. She challenged me again, and I continued to lie until I was nearly purple. Finally she gave up and sent us to meet the janitor at the bathroom, where we helped "clean up that other girl's mess" by wiping down mirrors and sinks.

That teacher knew I was a liar. My friends knew I was lying. I knew I was the dirtiest of liars, and I also knew that they all knew it, *but I didn't back down.* (I am still horrified by that behavior, by the way, but truth is truth, and I do my damnedest to tell it fully, accurately, and bluntly these days, lest I fall off the wagon again.)

Joseph never backed down, either. He may have slipped up a few times, may have said some things that he later recanted (likely during some of his more self-aggrandizing moments), or done some things in the name of God that proved unfeasible, but he *always* backed his own stories. He always *insisted* he was telling the truth, and he stuck to his story until it killed him.

Spit wads and martyrdom are two *very* different things, of course, but to a compulsive liar, the principle remains the same. You do what you need to do, say what you need to say, and become who you need to become in order to maintain the lie.

If the lie brings you attention, love, devotion, fame, glory, or in this case, all of the above, it's all the more important to maintain it. (It's arguably even MORE important to maintain a lie if the lie brings you either converts, a la "Lying for the Lord", or spiritual comfort, a la cognitive dissonance. Welcome to my world.)

Joseph Smith was also an author, like me. Though Mormons love to insist that he is a translator, he himself listed his own name at the beginning of the original Book of Mormon translation as "author and proprietor."

The very next edition of the BoM is missing that particular gem.

(Note: Joseph sent some of his buddies to Canada to attempt to sell the copyright to the Book of Mormon at one point, and it did not sell. Unfortunate, really, because if it had, it is highly unlikely that it would have then laid the foundation for this religion.)

People love to talk about how difficult it is to write a book, and how impossible it would be to put out a first draft and pass it off as a historical and scriptural work. Joseph, however, was remarkably creative, had lots of fictional works and tall tales to draw from (including Ethan Smith's View of the Hebrews and Solomon Spaulding's Manuscript Found), and clearly had access to the King James Bible, a book from which entire chapters were borrowed (mostly Isaiah). (Note: the KJV has numerous translation errors that made it, verbatim, into the BoM. If Smith was inspired rather than plagiarizing, wouldn't those errors have been corrected?)

As an author myself, it is not difficult to imagine Joseph sitting alone on the other side of a curtain from his scribe, his scriptures open, maps and legal documents and books all around him on the table and wall, inventing place names and people based on minor changes to words on those maps and in those documents, and, when especially bored, burned out, or out of sorts, flipping to Isaiah and plagiarizing the hell out of a dozen scriptural sections. (Yes, Joseph "translated" aloud to a scribe…from behind a curtain. It's a big like having the Dragon computer program! MAN, I could get so much more written that way!)

Additionally, we do NOT have the Book of Mormon's first draft. No one does. If we compare the first printing, however, with the current edition of the Book of Mormon, or what modern-day president of the church Ezra Taft Benson called "the most perfect book on the face of the earth and the keystone of our religion," there are glaring differences. (Don't take my word for it; hop online and do a search. It won't take but a second, and you'll find a host of websites that will demonstrate the 3,000 + differences for you.) Joseph Smith, then, is no different than the unfortunate majority of self-publishers today, passing off crap as good reading, and using his friends and scribes as his editors and proofers, to front the money to print the book, and then as his book-buyers. (I will undoubtedly be accused of three of the four elements of self-publishing listed above, but not the last: none of my LDS friends will likely ever read this...)

Joseph was also unequivocally a sex addict, and like any rock star, used his position to take full advantage of the women he desired. In the LDS church we are taught that Joseph married and adored Emma Smith. We *never* hear about the 30-some other women he married and...let's stick with the word "adored", shall we? My sweet Relief Society President? When I told her that I was upset by Joseph's polygamy and polyandry, she immediately and sternly denied it had ever happened, she having also attended BYU without ever learning that Joseph actually practiced what he preached.

Brodie goes into great detail about Joseph's other women – and Emma's reaction thereto – so I won't bother, but suffice it to say that when I learned he had married a couple teenage sisters behind his wife's back, bedded them both, and finally got his wife to approve of the marriages, remarrying them with the express order that they not reveal they were *already* married to (and had consummated their marriages with) him, I was, shall we say, dismayed. Emma had been through a hell of a lot during the course of their marriage thus far, including losing some of her children, and this particular story just made me ill. (PS: D&C 132 states that one of the qualifications for taking another wife is getting the first wife's approval. Hmm.)

Realizing that Joseph participated in polyandry also made me ill. At least 11 of his wives were *already married*, meaning that he would summon them for sex and send them right back home to their husbands and families. Imagine being one of those husbands, or a child belonging to one of those couples. Dear god, it's obscene. (D&C 132 also states that the new wife must be a virgin, but these ladies were married. Hmm.)

I was made *further* ill when I walked in to my in-laws' living room and found them watching an LDS film about Emma, which proved to be such horrendous propaganda that I had to leave the house for fear I'd say something I could not take back. (Interestingly enough, the film starred a very self-important girl with whom I had attended BYU. Odd to see her playing a super-righteous pioneer!)

(Note: Fanny Alger was likely Smith's first polygamous wife, the 16 year-old housemaid to the Smith family. By all accounts, Emma found the two in a compromising situation in their barn, and the "polygamy is restored!" revelation emerged from there.)

Joseph used polygamy to justify his sex addiction, and his position as prophet to ensure he would have a steady stream of income without ever having to do a day's *real* work. (Like most modern-day Mormons, it appears Joseph was a get-rich-quick schemer, and is the likely foundation for the LDS get-rich-quick obsession.) He was a gold digger, true, but not necessarily because he believed he was capable of finding gold; instead people who wanted him to find gold paid him to stare at his magical seer stones to see (or use his divining stick to divine) where buried treasure might be located. (The church, by the way, teaches that Joseph had a few little "dalliances" as a young man, but is quick to point out he was never *convicted* of swindling the people…only trying to.)

He also insisted, via the "Lord's command", that others house and feed him and his family, promising that those who helped out would be "blessed." (Apparently what it *was* like to be a Mormon remains what it *is* like to be a Mormon.) Eventually tithing became law, and Joseph was able to use tithing money to build the Mansion House in Nauvoo, Illinois. It was a grand building, housing both visiting dignitaries and Joseph's insanely large family of mostly wives, many of whom he claimed were only his wards when he spoke of them to friends, guests, and, of course, Emma. The Mansion House housed a bar, as well, and the booze was free-flowing. (Tithing – by revelation – was also used to build the Nauvoo House, a building which remained unfinished.)

Contrary to the Word of Wisdom, Joseph Smith was a fan of alcohol, and enjoyed some wine in Carthage jail shortly before he was murdered. (He also sent out for tobacco – a cigar, specifically – for Willard Richards for the sake of calming his stomach, but I think I mentioned that earlier.) This tends to shake people's testimonies when they first hear of it – it, too, is not something that is never taught – but the cognitive dissonance takes over and we Mormons dismiss it as perfectly fine "because the Word of Wisdom hadn't been made a commandment yet." So Joseph, who received *direct* revelation from God that alcohol was not to be ingested, enjoyed it anyway because God wasn't serious yet, right?

Riiiiiight.

But God *was* serious when He gave Lehi the same dream that Joseph's father, Joseph Smith, Sr. had had about the Tree of Life, as detailed in the book of Nephi. Or was it, He gave Joseph Smith, Sr. the same dream Lehi had? I forget. Either way, Lucy Mack Smith, Joseph's mother, discusses in her son's biography her husband's dream about a tree of life and the path to it, albeit in far more simplistic terms than the detailed imagery used in Lehi's dream.

One of my biggest shocks was learning that Joseph translated the gold plates *not* with the Urim and Thummim, as we are taught in church, but by putting his magic gold-digging seer stone into his hat and sticking his face in the hat. Additionally, the plates he was translating by staring at the rock in his hat were "buried in the woods".

They weren't even in the room.

So often in church teaching aids, we see illustrations of a bunch of golden pages bound by big u-shaped clasps, Joseph staring down at them through eyeglasses of sorts attached to a type of Old Testament breastplate (all marked "artist's rendition of the Urim and Thummim"), sharing his translation to someone sitting across the table busily jotting everything down with a quill pen. Just about the only correct feature in that image, it turns out, is the quill pen…and even that's up in the air. Instead, Joseph sat on the other side of a curtain with his face in a hat, or wandered about the room behind the curtain, making the floorboards creak. (Again, how I wish I could write a book purely by recitation! Someone find me a scribe…or buy me Dragon!)

Most important, though, is that the likelihood of the existence of *any* plates is *nil*.

No plates. *Ever.*

In fact, we seekers discover in our studies that Joseph bragged of having filled a bag with sand, stuffed it in a box, and wrapped he box in cloth, telling people God told him not to show anyone the gold plates lest He smite them…and then Joseph offered to give them a peek. He later laughed as he described how they ran from the room.

THE PLATES NEVER EXISTED. Worse, the three and the eight witnesses to the plates listed in the scriptures (who famously never recanted their stories) had a hard time signing the document presented at the beginning of the BoM (that Smith wrote for them to sign!) because they "saw" the plates, we discover, with their *spiritual eyes.*

In other words, they either hallucinated, or they dreamt up the Emperor's new clothes. Either way, no one has ever seen the *actual* plates, and considering *Joseph attempted to pay a metal worker back east to create a set that he could pass off as the plates* (and charge people to view!), in all likelihood those plates – the reason for the Book of Mormon's existence – *never existed at all.*

Know what else didn't exist? Gold in Salem. I had never recalled reading D&C section 111 in church, seminary, or at BYU. I read it on my own, of course, but dismissed it as just some random early-church stuff. At first glance it appears to be God telling Joseph to take a couple people with him to Salem, where he will receive money for and in behalf of the church. That's about all there is to the section; it's really quite short. God also has no further comment about the incident, as evidenced by the lack of any other reference to the situation in any other section of the D&C.

The rest of the story, of course, is more interesting. Having been *assured by God* that there was gold waiting in Salem, Joseph took a couple friends gold-digging, telling them that an old gold-digging associate had informed him there was a large trove of buried gold under a barn there. All Joseph had to do was go dig it up. Needless to say, there was no gold, Joseph and his friends returned home empty-handed, and God – not for the first time in the LDS faith – was *wrong*. The section is still there, and you can find it on LDS.org. Though time has erased the truth behind section 111, history has not.

Nothing, not history, not time, not God Himself, can erase section 132 of the D&C, either. I wish that, for just this moment, you could see section 132 in my childhood scriptures. It has a series of rather garish red hearts drawn around its introduction; I put them there myself using a red scripture marker when I was about 16 years old. In seminary, you see, we learn that 132 is the Celestial Marriage section. It reveals the celestial ordinance and structure of temple marriage, and is everything that us girls were taught to dream about. Trouble is, I don't know that any of us ever read anything but the verses we were made to memorize for "scripture chase."

Each year seminary students have the opportunity to seek and find one of a hundred scriptures taught during four years of seminary, twenty-five per year, as part of a contest to see who has best-learned the scriptures.

When I finally took a step back from section 132 and read it in its entirety, putting myself in Emma's place as I did so, I wept. There is *nothing* spiritual, beautiful, or redeeming about it. It is, instead, a personal threat from Joseph to Emma, demanding she accept wife after wife for her husband, and promising her utter destruction should she refuse. It also originally stated that celestial marriage isn't just temple marriage; to qualify as a *celestial* marriage, there must be one husband and multiple wives. Period, the end.

This marriage I'm in that I have dreamed of since the time I was old enough to fall in love with Disney movies? It's not celestial and won't get us to the Celestial Kingdom. Not until my husband takes another wife or two in the afterlife, anyway. We will have to be polygamous to get there. For more on the absolute horror that is polygamy, please read both Ann-Eliza Webb and Fanny Stenhouse.

*Note: I adore Fanny. We're two peas in a pod, and if there IS an afterlife, she and I will definitely hang out. Occasionally you hear of people feeling a connection to historical figures across decades and centuries. When reading Fanny's work, and for the first time in my life, I felt that connection. It was as though I could reach through some sort of inter-dimensional curtain and take her hand. (I know. Mormon, remember?) Her way of thinking, her tangents – like this one right now – and her writing style are all ME. If Regina Samuelson had lived in the mid-to-late 1800's, she'd have been Fanny Stenhouse. Fanny made me weep, sigh, shake my head, and laugh out loud. She, like Ann-Eliza, is an amazingly accessible writer telling her own story in an autobiography that, from time to time, I actually had to put down, I was so shaken.

At one point I shared with my husband a few lines from Fanny's book that were so utterly *me*, I hardly knew how to process it. This led to one of the most emotionally debilitating realizations of my entire life thus far: Fanny (and Ann-Eliza and Kay and Park and Lee and Fawn, etc.) wrote her book to prevent the existence of people like me. It's not that she wants me dead, or wished I had not been born; she wrote her book in a

84

desperate attempt to awaken others to the fallacies and horrors of the LDS Church and what it does to its adherents. She wrote with the hope that Mormonism would have died out long ago, so that by the time I came along, there would be no chance of my suffering from it, as well. I wish more people would read her work, but because the LDS Church still exists, and because it produces people like me, I write to you now to carry on Fanny's message.*

Fanny and Ann-Eliza's books are shocking depictions of life in polygamy, both surprisingly modern, and contain accounts of all sorts of atrocities committed in the name of the LDS faith. At one point Ann-Eliza notes that there are things she has seen that no decent woman could ever speak on, (Fanny concludes with a similar sentiment,) and declines to provide these unmentionable details. We are left to wonder: what sort of extreme squalor were some of these women and children forced to live in? What sort of rape, abuse, and sexual torture was used against some of these ladies *in the name of God*? What sort of deviant behaviors were displayed by these men, and what type of perversions did they demand their wives participate in? Oft times multiple wives were required to live in one single household consisting of one solitary room. What horrors were they and their children forced to witness or endure that women like Ann-Eliza and Fanny refused even to suggest?

The mind shudders to think on it.

Smith himself was an example of at least a few of those horrors, none of them discussed in church, of course. Having secretly married Eliza Snow and installed her in the Mansion House, Joseph went about his business, never revealing the marriage to Emma. Emma found out quick enough: Eliza was pregnant with Joseph's baby. Upon discovery of the deceit, Emma allegedly tore Eliza from her room and threw her down the stairs at the front of the house and out into the snow, clad only in her nightgown. Eliza miscarried, but Emma felt no pity and would not allow her back into the house. Eliza was lucky to have miscarried, it seems; abortions were all the rage in Nauvoo, with Joseph and others sending their as-yet-undiscovered extra wives to visit the town abortion doctor, John C. Bennett, who made a substantial living providing his services to the surrounding polygamous folk. (So much for life being sacred.)

Most notoriously, though, Emma allegedly tried to kill her husband, poisoning him (likely with arsenic) to the point of being gravely ill. Tit for tat, section 132 advises Emma "not to drink that which her husband offered her," or something to that effect. In other words, Joseph was on to the plot of his non-compliant wife, and was warning her that he knew what was going on, and if she didn't cut it out, it wasn't GOD who would destroy her, but Joseph himself.

But that was the sort of man Joseph was. The sort who wrote himself into the "inspired" version of the Bible. You read that right. As a teen I was perplexed by the JST – the Joseph Smith Translation – in the back of my Bible. Large sections of scripture had been "restored" to their "original" state, but even then, I wasn't buying it; all those restorations seemed more like "fixes" for inconvenient sections and doctrines in the Old and New Testament. Most baffling, however, was a rewritten section of Genesis that makes Jesus the Savior, and Joseph – *by name* – the Restorer. (Genesis 50:33 in the Joseph Smith Translation. Seriously, look it up on lds.org.)

Anything inconvenient could be adjusted, so long as the name of God was invoked. Take the original 116 page manuscript of the BoM, known as the book of Lehi. When it was taken by Martin Harris to show his wife and alleviate her concerns over his investment in the project *and then the manuscript disappeared*, (history assumes that Harris's wife destroyed it,) God rebuked Joseph (rather mildly) and told him he would not be permitted to re-translate the book, lest Joseph's enemies pull out the 116 page document later to show the world that the two translations were significantly different. *Luckily*, God announced that the same general story of Lehi was retold in a condensed form by Lehi's son, Nephi, so Lehi's words would not be lost, and Joseph could continue translating from the Book of Nephi on. Also, God explained that He had known this was going to happen ahead of time, hence the reason He personally instructed Nephi to re-explain his father's situation, background, and faith. All was not lost, and the book of Nephi was translated and completed with all due haste and remarkable speed.

Before you roll your eyes and I entirely lose you to the stupidity of the general Mormon membership, I think this is a good time to remind you of cognitive dissonance, of the horrible reality facing those who try to leave the faith, and of our absolute desperation to believe what we've been taught, *even if it makes absolutely no sense at all*. Please pity us. This is no way to live, and coming out of it is pure and absolute agony. I, for one, did my utmost to shrug off and ignore the existence of the original 116 page manuscript, and even remember excusing myself to the bathroom as a teenager when it became a topic of Sunday school class discussion. Ignoring was okay; disbelief was not an option.

We…need…*help*. (Psychological help, and general understanding. I'm pursuing the psychological help portion *now*, and my official diagnosis is "Adjustment Disorder.")

Most disarming of all this ridiculousness, though, is the book of Abraham in the Pearl of Great Price. I was eight years old when I discovered the facsimiles in the back of my baptismal scriptures. They depicted things like an Egyptian trying to sacrifice Abraham on a big stone slab, and God on His throne in his Kolob home. Each picture was tagged by numbers, and each number contained an explanation of the image courtesy of Joseph Smith.

Those pictures were fascinating to my eight year-old mind. Abraham had been ordered to kill Isaac after he himself had almost been sacrificed? God lived on a planet called Kolob? That girlie-looking figure is actually *God*? (It wasn't until I was about 14 that I thought, "HOLY HELL, IS THAT AN ERECTION IN MY SCRIPTURES?" Sure enough, one of the characters has one!) Oh, and…the character with the dog head isn't an Egyptian god, it's an *LDS symbol*, meaning the *Egyptians knew about the "original" faith?*

I also immediately started searching the pictures for the marks I had seen on my parents garments – "V", "–", and "L", or a compass, line, and square of Masonic descent – but couldn't find them anywhere. I figured they were somehow embedded in the images, and I just wouldn't understand it until I went through the temple. As I aged, I became more and more fascinated with Egyptology, sure that the ancient Egyptians had known all sorts of gospel secrets and other things we couldn't possibly imagine. I believed for a time that the pyramids were the "V" symbol upside down, that the stone altars on which the dead (presumably) were laid for burial preparation were the "–" symbol, and that maybe the Sphinx was a backward "L". I became more and more excited for the temple, sure that some of the images in the book of Abraham referred to the things I would learn there, and maybe the outstretched hands of some of the characters, or their headdresses, *something*, would seem more familiar once I learned the signs and tokens required to pass the sentinels guarding the way back to my Heavenly Father.

Instead I learned that Joseph "translated" the book of Abraham from some papyri that fell into his hands from a roving collection of Egyptian artifacts, and that they had been "proven" – some 40 years shy of the Rosetta Stone giving up its secrets – to have actually been written by the hand of Abraham thousands of years before! Later, of course, I learned that science had determined that Joseph Smith's translation was preposterous; the documents, found in the 1960's, were actually incredibly common funerary papyri, and Joseph Smith's facsimiles contained glaring inaccuracies and potential alterations to the typical pictures contained on a funerary papyrus. (Google it.) It seems that the papyrus containing the image of Abraham about to be sacrificed had a hole in the area where the executioner's head was supposed to be, and Joseph had penciled in the face of a black man, when in fact the image should have been of a long-snouted dog. The explanations given for the small urns under the stone slab were all debunked; clearly, the urns were for the preservation of organs for mummification, one for the heart, one for the brain, etc. The image of God that looked like a woman *was* a woman. Every single item in the facsimiles that I had studied for years, that had held my interest during long sacrament meetings when nothing else would, was bullshit, plain and simple.

That wasn't Joseph's only "oops". Though I had never been told in church that the Pearl of Great Price – which, by the way, is a foundation of the temple endowment – had been debunked, I had never even *heard* of the Kinderhook plates. They were a set of fraudulent plates assembled by Joseph's opponents, covered in nonsensical chicken scratch, and presented to the prophet to translate these newly-discovered "scriptures". Joseph was excited, announced he could indeed translate them, and set to work. We have no idea if he ever succeeded outside of his announcement (via his secretary) that the plates were written by a descendant of Ham "through the loins of Pharaoh, King of Egypt." Though lost, the church published facsimiles of them and included them as an ancient reference of sorts until they were debunked in 1980, at which time the church disavowed them and pointed out that Joseph had never actually begun any sort of translation.

At some point, of course, the final coffin nail is pounded in.

I can't say that the Pearl of Great Price and the Kinderhook plates provided that final pounding for me, unfortunately, but I sometimes think, somewhere in the darkest recesses of my mind, their hammer clang reverberated most loudly.

The historical Mormon Church brings forth *lots* of cringe-worthy items. Attending the baptism of a Catholic friend's baby a couple years back, I was forced to look at my own children and assess their innocence, realizing my firstborn had a little less than two years to go before baptism. I stared at my friend's baby, sick to think that he would be in any way accountable for his "sins" or anyone else's, Adam and Eve included. I then stared for a time at my own child, suddenly just as sick to think that my sweet, innocent, developing babe, then six, would be considered accountable for sin in God's eyes in such an incredibly short time. Eight seemed so young; eight *is* so young. Yet, the moment my children turned eight, they would magically go from perfectly innocent to miserably sinful. Hitting your sibling one day was cause for parental correction; hitting them the next would deny you entrance into the Kingdom of God unless you "brought forth fruits meet for repentance."

It was Joseph Smith who introduced eight as God's cut-off, and Smith who introduced us to the endowment ceremony that would allow us to return to God. If ever you were curious about the endowment ceremony but didn't want an internet script play-by-play, you could easily get the feel from any documentary on Masonry. (Two birds, one stone!) So intensely similar are the two ceremonies that my husband and I were absolutely shocked as we watched a Masonry documentary on television. Thankfully, the threat of Blood Atonement no longer applies in the temple ceremony, so I can tell you that with relative confidence that my throat will not be slit.

What is Blood Atonement? A concept introduced in the early LDS church requiring the shedding of an individual's blood (read: the taking of their life) in specific circumstances. It was a multi-faceted concept, but in brevity: according to the LDS gospel, certain sins – murder, adultery, etc – are not covered by the sacrifice of Jesus Christ and must be atoned for personally in order to receive redemption. Additionally, the revealing of temple covenants used to be strictly forbidden, under penalty of death.

THIS WAS ACTUALLY PRACTICED IN THE EARLY CHURCH. There are numerous reported cases of suicide and murder related to the "doctrine" of blood atonement, and interestingly, it still applies in at least one sense: Mormons today support the death penalty. We believe, whether we think of it that way or not, that Christ's sacrifice is somehow insufficient to cover the sin of shedding innocent blood, and that the blood of the murderer must in turn be shed if the individual is to have any hope of attaining any sort of glory. There is a rather gory account in early church history of such a thing (albeit not in any authorized church history book!): a woman committed adultery, and once discovered, sat penitently on her husband's lap while he, in turn, slit her throat from ear to ear. Another such account was of a man who felt his sins to be so grievous, he disemboweled himself while his brethren stood by. They, in turn, cleaned up after the suicide and gave him a proper, "now-deserved" burial.

In the original endowment ceremony, handshakes and signs were accompanied by additional signs demonstrating the penalty attached to revealing that particular part of the covenant. These included slitting your throat, having your organs ripped from your body, and disembowelment. These were removed from the endowment ceremony in 1990, and it just so happens that an in-law of mine was among the very last to receive his endowments while the death-covenants still remained. He was understandably mortified, and claims it was like pulling teeth to get him to go back again.

More amazing to me is that my husband's parents, some of the most righteous, stalwart people I have ever met, received their endowments (and returned regularly to the temple) during a time when the aforementioned items were still attached to the ceremony. I struggle to imagine my ultra-Mormon mother-in-law figuratively slitting her own throat. Most amazing of all, though, is that my OWN parents, converts to the church, ever felt they made the right decision by becoming Mormon, going to the temple, and raising their children in the faith when they, too, received their endowments during a time when they were required to simulate tearing out their own organs. (When I asked Mom how they could keep going after that, she explained that, betwixt Dad's work, their home-buying, and the arrival of babies, they honestly hadn't had much opportunity to return to the temple until after the death-covenants were gone.)

The temple threw me for a loop my first time through. Whether they were able to go regularly to the temple or not, the fact that my parents stuck with it says something.

I'm just not sure what.

*   *   *

I don't know that I've yet pointed out another odd thing about my parents and the church: my mother is a die-hard 1960's feminist. (Or at least, she was. I don't know many uber-feminists who ended up stay-home moms.) She raised us with an eye toward education and career, and I well-remember her telling us about a conversation she had with a high priest on the phone one day:

"Hello?"

"Hi, this is Brother Stake Guy; is your husband there?"

"Not at the moment. May I take a message?"

He paused, apparently deliberating. "That's okay, I can call back."

"Is there anything you'd like me to tell him?"

More hesitation. "Are you sure you can be accurate with the message?"

If only that man had known Mom. Instead, he had to reap the whirlwind. "Gee, I don't know," she said. "If you'll just let me go get my crayon and a piece of construction paper, I'm fairly certain I can spell it out phonetically. *Even the big words.*"

Silence on the other end of the phone, and then, "Okay. Please tell him there's a high council meeting Thursday night at 7."

"Oh," my mom assured him, "he'll get the message." I'm sure she couldn't stop herself. "Next time you need to tell him something of such magnitude, though, be sure to let me know when I pick up the phone so I can sharpen my crayon."

How the hell did my mother ever make it as a Mormon?

Having now read Brodie, Webb, Stenhouse, Beck, and Burningham, I wonder that any woman ever makes it. The degree to which the LDS faith has been infected by the early saints' polygamy and misogyny is still somewhat beyond my comprehension. It wasn't until I accepted my own disbelief that I finally realized how deeply members' disregard for women has affected me personally. I'll offer far more detail in that realm once we reach the "confessional" portion of this book; for the time being I focus solely on the irrefutable evidence (discovered through my studies) that the aforementioned items – polygamy and misogyny – existed in the early church in spades, building a foundation for today.

It all goes back to Adam and Eve, but not the version you know. Mormons believe Genesis was inappropriately tweaked to omit certain important facts and ideas. The Pearl of Great Price offers a new version of the Adam and Eve story, giving rise to the idea that Adam did not commit an "original sin." Instead, Mormons see it as a transgression. Because Adam didn't know the difference between good and bad, he could not have sinned, only transgressed. Eve's a little different, though. According to the LDS gospel, Satan had told her enough that she more or less understood what she was getting herself into, and then, thanks to her opened eyes, was able to play on Adam's emotions and get him to eat naughty fruit, too, pointing out that if she was forced out of the Garden, they could never reproduce. Eve was not only a sinner, she was a temptress. That's not what the story screams, of course, and Eve is not demonized, but is instead recognized as the Mother of Man. Though she may not be portrayed in Sunday school as a seductive manipulator, the sense is the same. Also, she is made to be the breeder in the marriage relationship while Adam is the breadwinner, dependent upon him for her protection and support, and required to tend and nurture his seed.

PS: Speaking of "seed", remember the garish green apron from the temple? Satan tells Adam and Eve – and those of us in the endowment session – to cover up with the leaf-apron. *We never again take off the item Satan instructs us to wear.*

Anyone else squirming in their seats?

Back to the topic at hand: Mormon women are not set up to be equal partners with their husbands. Some of us pull it off anyway, but as you'll see in later chapters, many don't.

While the Pearl of Great Price makes women into over-educated temptresses, the BoM has a serious lack of women throughout…almost as though we didn't exist. The only woman I can recall at the moment is Sariah, Lehi's wife, famous for murmuring (read: grumbling behind God's back). She was a faithless nag, regularly corrected by both her husband Lehi and son Nephi.

Nephi married someone – his wife is actually mentioned at one point – but if she had a name, we'll never know it. King Lamoni's wife is mentioned, too, but apparently queens don't merit naming. There are some women in the wilderness, I think, and women who made food and clothing for…someone…meaning the BoM contains primarily wild women and housewives! The only other reference to women in the BoM of which I'm aware is to the mothers of the Stripling Warriors, a group of brave and righteous men who credited their devotion to God to their dear, sweet moms. (All moms melt when their sons expresses their love, but even as a kid I thought those particular scriptures were meant to underpin the need for moms to remain in the home, as opposed to letting their own stripling warriors learn about atheism from a daycare.) It's nigh unto impossible to find a female hero in the Book of Mormon, which is why we all fall back on loving the Striplings' moms, reinforcing our desire to become mothers ourselves.

Speaking of mothers, it is a well-known fact in the LDS church that we have a Heavenly Mother. We don't pray to her, don't speak of her, and though God's name has been revealed to us – Elohim, for those interested, and yes, I *know* Elohim's etymology, but like everything else, I swept its "nonsensical" nature under my bedroom rug – we are told He will never reveal His wife's name. She's so wonderful and sweet and precious, He couldn't bear to hear her name sullied, so He won't tell anyone what it is.

(I wonder if it's the same name they gave me in the temple?!)

While still a child, I told my mom that I knew about Heavenly Mother, and I sort of wanted to pray to Her, since I was pretty sure no one else ever did. Mom told me to have at it; showing our Heavenly Mother respect and deference via prayer couldn't possibly hurt. I gave it a shot that next week, but when I mentioned it to my primary teacher and she freaked out, I gave up.

I asked in my teenage Sunday school class once if *anyone* had ever known Heavenly Mother's name, and my teacher replied with a far more chilling counter-question: rather than Her name, maybe I should be asking how many of Her are there? The boys in the class reacted in a predictably excited way, but I was thunderstruck: *God had more than one wife?!*

Even better, I learned at BYU that Brigham Young claimed both God *and* Christ are polygamists, right along with Brigham. So not only did Jesus marry Mary Magdalene, the church's informal position (suggested, but not preached), I guess if Brigham was right and you also have to add the other Mary and Martha to the mix, He really got around!

The proposition was horrifying beyond what my mind could handle, both as a teen, and at BYU. (Note: BYU was named for Brigham Young, though he very strongly discouraged the saints from attaining anything beyond the most basic education, even as he sent his own children to East Coast universities!) Again, cognitive dissonance came to my rescue. Furthermore, I'd ignored how obscene the suggestion of a polygamist God and Savior were for so long, by the time I was married, I could actually joke that maybe my husband and I *weren't* spiritual brother and sister in the pre-existence; maybe we were spiritual *half* brother and sister. (The concept that we are all spirit sons and daughters of our Heavenly Father has always upset me, by the way; that means that this man I married here on Earth during my human experience is actually one of billions of my *brothers*. Really?)

What does this mean God thinks women are good for, according to LDS history? Mating, breeding, and house-keeping.

Only a couple more things really bother me about the early church...enough to say "I'm done", anyway. (Plenty bothers me, but it's already been said by others far more thorough than I, and again, I STRONGLY advocate reading Fanny Stenhouse, Fawn Brodie, and Ann-Eliza Webb if you're interested in seeing exactly how deep the proverbial rabbit hole goes.) A major one for me is plains-crossing, particularly involving handcart companies.

Perhaps it was because I was raised by converts, or because I didn't pay close enough attention in seminary or my D&C classes at BYU, but I never understood exactly how many treks were made from the East to the Salt Lake Valley until recently. Some were incredibly easy (comparatively), made in covered wagons in a few short weeks. Others were pure torture, with families pulling handcarts and limited to nearly no supplies for months of trekking through cold and snow. The hardest and longest of these journeys were often made by immigrants who had, only months or even weeks before, made the Atlantic crossing in steerage quarters. I had always chalked up those agonies to amazing tests of pioneer faith, lauding the pioneers for their shining beacons of testimony.

Set aside the fact that they were duped into the religion, duped into selling all their belongings (and giving over the proceeds of their sales to the church for "safe-keeping"), duped into crossing a forbidding landscape through territory they didn't know during untenable seasonal weather, duped into believing rumors of polygamy in Utah were just *rumors*, and for just a moment examine Brigham Young, then prophet.

Webb's book reveals Young for the tyrant he was: 99% of what Webb has to say shows up *nowhere* in church history books or manuals. If you want to read the unsanitized version, you have to go directly to the journals and histories kept by some of the people directly involved with the nightmare that was Brigham Young. I had always thought of him as the sweet old grandpa-type, kind and generous in his willingness to marry and support (by some accounts) 55 women who "needed" a husband.[iii]

Turns out he was a money-grubbing, self-important misogynist. He and Heber Kimball, another early church leader, are both quoted as having referred to their wives as both cows or heifers *and* as belongings. Young lived like a king off the tithing fund, often relegating his less-adored wives to providing financially for themselves and their children. Ann-Eliza reports that she believed he was worth $600,000/year, which, even by today's standards, is an awful lot of money...and while she was, indeed, provided with a home for her and her children, she was forced to let rooms and run her home as a boarding house in order to support herself and her family. Every time Young had nearly emptied the church coffers, he sent another group of men on missions seeking converts, and they said what they had to say to convince people to join the church and transplant themselves, their families, and their money to Salt Lake City. (When Young owed a large chunk of money to the Salt Lake "gentiles" – the LDS term for non-members – he would head to the Tithing Office with his debts and have the office administrator cut him a check to meet those debts, chalking it up to payment for "services rendered"...sometimes to the tune of hundreds of thousands of dollars. No joke. Read Stenhouse and Webb.)

Remember, I was raised to think of Young as a prophet. Keepign that in mind, at first Young used tithing money to help converts make their way to the valley, but it quickly became too expensive to import tithe payers to add to the tithing fund. Eventually Young introduced the Perpetual Emigration Fund.

Folks of today's church will instantly recall the Perpetual EDUCATION Fund, introduced during General Conference a few years back, allowing young people to attend college on the cheap, so long as they paid it forward. Original monies came from the generosity of college-educated Mormons. To this day my husband and I regularly receive calls from BYU requesting we donate to the PEF.

Members were strongly encouraged to give any and all they could spare – *after* the payment of tithes and offerings, of course – to the Emigration Fund to assist their newly-converted brothers and sisters in making their way to Deseret, the Mormon name for their Utah community.

People gave and gave, as they always did when their prophet ordered it, and the immigrants kept coming. Eventually, though, the crossings were again deemed too expensive, and Young assembled a plan to have immigrant converts cross the plains using handcarts. They were cheap to build, would not require the purchase of beasts of burden, and would still hold "everything" a family required for their plains-crossing…so long as they limited themselves to 17 pounds of belongings per person, *including food*. The accounts of some of those crossings – particularly those of the Willie and Martin handcart companies – are unimaginably horrific and heartbreakingly tragic. Vast numbers of people died clinging to their false faith, and vast numbers more were disheartened and disgusted by the church and the rampant polygamy they found upon arriving in Utah, but were too destitute to return home. There were those who did save money, apostatize, and then tried to leave, but more often than not their bodies were found some distance from Salt Lake, having been "murdered by Indians".

*Tangent warning: Danites! The Danites were Joseph (and later Brigham's) "avenging angels", as they were called, and were basically a secret police-like task force. They included the likes of Porter Rockwell, bodyguard to Joseph Smith and failed assassin of Missouri Governor Lilburn Boggs, and Bill Hickman, bodyguard to Brigham Young (Hickman's autobiography is absolutely TERRIFYING!), and the Danites were always available to tend to whatever issue might need tending. In the words of Bill Hickman, he and the Danites were there to do as directed by Brigham Young: "Use [them] up."

Read: *kill people*.

Yes, the prophet had a squad of assassins. Type "Danites" into the search area of Wikipedia.org and brace yourself. Note: the Wikipedia article mentions the "whistling and whittling brigade", a group of men and boys who would follow strangers around the city of Nauvoo whistling as they walked. If the stranger did not leave, the group would then begin whittling sticks with their knives, most often in a tight circle around the stranger, the ends of the sticks being whittled brought incredibly close to the stranger's face. Most strangers made a beeline for the city limits, you can imagine.*

Back to the point, though:

Members have made a movie about the Martin and Willie handcart expeditions, two of the most disastrous. Even the title of the movie – "17 Miracles" – is propaganda, the spin being a focus on the faith of the pioneers, while the one man saying "This is insane! If we leave now and winter hits, we'll die!" appears almost criminal in his doubting. It doesn't matter how it is spun, though; some of the "trials" endured by the pioneers would never have existed had it not been for Young's greed, greed, and more greed. (For more on those trials, read Fanny Stenhouse's Tell it All; she receives a letter from her dear friend Mary Burton, who was a member of the Willie Handcart Company, and Mary offers a firsthand account of the journey. I have never yet been able to read it without weeping.) Between the handcart companies and the Mountain Meadows Massacre alone, Brigham Young has more blood on his hands than Jim Jones.

By the way, there are some excellent objective books available on the Mountain Meadows Massacre that are worth perusing if you'd like to know more about the depth of the early church's depravity. Just google it.

My one final early church gripe: there's no proof for the Book of Mormon ANYWHERE. The Smithsonian has had to go so far as to tell inquiring church members, fueled by rumors in the church that the Smithsonian Institution uses the Book of Mormon as a historical guide, that they *in no way, shape, or form* recognize the Book of Mormon as *anything other than a religious text*. Period.

Why would they? Native Americans lack Jewish DNA, being more closely related to Mongolian land bridge travelers. Beit Lehi is *not* a hangout for Lehi's family in the African wilderness; it's a long-utilized compound in an area where "Lehi" is a not-uncommon name. And Chichen Itza? Tulum? Machu Picchu? All those beautiful Mayan, Aztec, and Incan cities, buildings, and artifacts? They were not Lamanite, Nephite, and Jaredite settlements called Bountiful, Zarahemla, and Jacobugath, and there were no steel weapons, bones, or "plates" buried in Hill Cumorah. I spoke to a Mayan tour guide about Tulum. (Mayans still exist, by the way; they hid underground for 200 years to avoid the Spaniards, and today number over 800,000 people living around the Yucatan peninsula. I asked our guide – half Mayan, half Mexican, and his name is Jorge, by the way – if he, like the LDS rumors I'd heard, was a Mormon, too. He laughed.

"I'm not Mormon, I'm MAYAN. Any Mayan who says otherwise has sold out."

....*And I quote.*

The Modern Church

Have you ever been to Utah? I don't mean to Park City to ski; I mean to visit Salt Lake City, or maybe down to Utah County, also known as Happy Valley. Utah is beautiful, has the most amazing sunsets I've ever seen, and offers just about every conceivable outdoor activity. It's also a giant theocracy full of Mormons that run the gamut from ultra-devout to ultra-anti. The vast majority of the populace appear related, like they've come from the same northern European country. To an outsider – particularly a non-Caucasian one – Utah is total culture shock.

Super-believers love Utah. To the rest of us – even Mormons only a state or two away – it's overwhelming. Rather like being a Catholic in Vatican City, I imagine; the church is often more culture than religion. BYU is infinitely worse: faith and culture are inseparable, and anyone not completely aligned with both, *and* in the manner their peers, professors, and religious leaders expect, will inevitably struggle.

Beautiful as Utah is, I could never raise children there. The culture demands non-believers convert. When that fails, non-believers are often ostracized. The culture also demands that believers believe in the proscribed fashion; those with beliefs outside the norm are also ostracized, berated, or defamed. Oddly, Utahns pride themselves on their open-mindedness, but when someone like Park Romney, cousin to Mitt Romney, apostatizes, the backlash is immediate. One need only read his book The Apostasy of a High Priest: The Sociology of an American Cult to see that he, too, met with the typical backlash to his unbelief. (Incidentally, if you are seeking a book that will explain the epistemology and sociology of Mormonism, his book is a revelation, and I highly recommend it. For further study of LDS psychology, read Lyndon Lamborn's Standing for Something More; it is an equally astute guide to the Mormon psyche.) It seems Park Romney's extended family has even gone so far as to ensure his grandchildren are never left unsupervised with grandpa...and his experience is not the exception.

Truly, one cannot imagine the journey ahead of an LDS apostate.

For those unaware, the church has 3.5 universities to its name: BYU in Provo, Utah, BYU-I in Rexburg, Idaho, and BYU Hawaii, plus Southern Virginia University which, while not officially a church school, has become *the* East Coast stomping ground for LDS college kids. Additionally, the church owns the LDS Business College in Salt Lake, and the vast majority of college students in Utah, including those attending USU, U of U, UVU (formerly UVSC), SUU, and Dixie College, are LDS.

Both my husband and I attended BYU in Provo, Utah, and our experiences were vastly different, primarily because I was single for the balance of my university experience, but my husband and I were already married when he attended BYU. In other words, I was still in the Meat Market, but my husband was allowed to head home after class and have as much sex as he desired…with me, of course. My time at university was based in part around trying to catch a husband. His time was devoted to his studies, the end goal being a well-paying job to provide the sole monetary support for his family.

A BYU education consists of standard general education classes, classes pertinent to your major, and 16 religion credits attained from 2-credit classes, preferably one class per semester for four years. The courses range from LDS Marriage and Family to 1st half of the Book of Mormon to 2nd half of the New Testament, Sharing the Gospel, and everything in between. Most of the professors are lifelong members with special qualifications in the Mormon apologist arena, and many pull double-duty as bishops or stake presidents of BYU student wards. Some are even lower-level general authorities.

It was at BYU that I learned of something called the "Second Anointing," a temple covenant above-and-beyond what we had all believed to be the be-all, end-all: marriage. While you can read about it online, it's basically an ordinance that "seals you up unto eternity, making your calling and election sure." Translation? If you've been selected for that ordinance, you're pretty much guaranteed your place in the Celestial Kingdom, and there really isn't much you can do to screw it up.

I first learned about the second anointing from my 2nd half New Testament professor, who suggested it was possible to "have your calling and election made sure while still in this life." Though he did not come right out and say it, he implied – *strongly* – that he himself (and his wife) had been so blessed. And how does one come to be selected for such a thing, considering how few members know it is even a possibility? The answer is one simple word: connections.

My father-in-law is one of the most righteous people I have *ever* met. Everything you could ever hope for in a husband, father, and father-in-law is part of this remarkable man. (I realize I may be biased, but markedly few people adore their in-laws, so if I can rave about him as his daughter-in-law, you can trust that he is truly a gem.) That said, I am convinced that he will never receive his second anointing, never become a general authority, never be called as a mission president, and will probably also never be made a stake president. Why? Not because he lacks devotion, is sinful, or is unwilling, but because he lacks *connections*. He doesn't live in Utah, isn't in a ward with a general authority, hasn't got a graduate degree, and doesn't have a bank account overflowing with funds generated by years of grand success in business. In short, he will have to *work* to make it to the Celestial Kingdom. There will be no second anointing forthcoming. Considering he is likely unaware that the potential for a second anointing even exists, this probably will never bother him. Still, for such a devout member of the LDS faith, I find his exclusion – intentional or otherwise – incredibly sad.

But there are lots of sad things – and people – in the modern church. Lots of confusion, too. Take missionaries. (More on them when the "red flag" section of this book comes up.) What happens when you throw two men together at the height of their sexuality – somewhere between 18 and 25, depending on when they have a chance to serve – for two years, swapping out companions every few months? A number of potentially *intensely* confusing things, all horrifying to church members:

- Homosexual desires can be introduced or strengthened, leading to possible incidents
- Masturbation can become obsessive, as can masturbation fodder (like a Victoria's Secret catalog), including pornography
- The sexual drive can be dampened or deadened if not properly utilized (hence the large numbers of sexually ambivalent 30-something virgins in the church)
- Young men may become desperate to marry too young and too quickly upon their return (after a probable adjustment period), eventually leading to divorce
- Sexual obsessions form around foreign women, leading to

missionaries sending for brides from their mission or deliberately seeking a bride from that culture to the exclusion of other women, making future divorce an utter nightmare for the wife and kids

Please keep in mind that the average white Utah Mormon is *terrified* of having a child who is gay, sex-obsessed, married outside their ethnicity, or who lacks an interest in breeding. Any of those items constitutes a crisis in a Mormon family. I repeat: *crisis*. Think disillusioned, devastated, nearly destroyed parents pleading with God for the child's salvation; siblings and extended family passing around accusations and rumors; friends and ward members shocked and distraught, attempting to comfort the grieving – yes, *grieving* – parents. It's a mess, and intensely sad for everyone involved…and for everyone who involved themselves.

Here I must confess, not to similar behavior, but to profound ignorance about something affecting at least 15% of the world's population. Until a few months ago, *I did not believe that geneticists had ever been able to offer any sort of proof that homosexuality is or could be genetic.* Like my fellow church members I had eagerly pointed out to everyone that there was no proof of a "gay" gene, and that, much like an alcoholic, I was certain that people could be born with a propensity toward a certain "sin," but that giving in to that propensity was a *choice*. I have actually seen a host of examples throughout my life to verify the accuracy of that belief, including sexually abused kids who "came out" years later, children who had trust issues with the opposite gender (thanks to strange parental relationships) who devoted themselves to same-sex relationships, and even men I'd dated who I was well-aware, thanks to dramatic physical indication, were interested in me physically, but who later announced they were gay. Additionally, I've had close friends who had been grossly mistreated by opposite-sex partners and had turned to their own gender for comfort and love, seeming to be sucked in to a new set of desires.

I view the world differently now, having finally shed my Mormon-colored glasses. There are those who are genetically heterosexual and cannot be swayed, those who are genetically homosexual and cannot be swayed, those that are one or the other, but remain bi-curious, and those that are genetically sexually ambivalent, content with either gender. I still maintain that people have a certain amount of control over both their sex- and relationship-partner decisions – specifically those who are bi-curious and those that are bisexual – but I can no longer claim that it is a choice. That would be like arguing that die-hard heterosexuals choose their straight-ness but *could* be gay, which, when intimated to a heterosexual alpha-male, is tantamount to blasphemy.

And so I must repent. **I humbly apologize to anyone I may have injured by suggesting that their wiring was anything other than wiring.** I humbly apologize for having voted in favor of both Prop 22 and Prop 8. *I truly did not understand.* (If *you* still require evidence, perform an internet search; any legitimately scientific website will provide it *in spades.*)

I did indeed vote, as suggested by my church, in favor of the aforementioned propositions. I also delivered pro-Prop 8 voting reminders around my local neighborhood and posted a "Protect Marriage" sign in our yard, and was horribly offended when a neighbor dared to call me a bigot.

Please understand: most active, faithful Mormons have likely *never been told that homosexuality is genetic*, and even if they have, they have been offered vast amounts of "evidence" that "no gay gene has ever been found." *They are truly unintentionally ignorant.* I say unintentionally because cognitive dissonance kicks in when the topic comes up, and they are so well trained in dismissing anything that does not mesh with their paradigm, that the possibility of a gay gene just doesn't compute. If there is no gay gene, homosexuality is relegated to "choice," and if it is a choice, one can make a different, more traditional (and more "acceptable") selection. Also, without a gay gene, gays, lesbians, bisexuals, and transgendered people are not viewed as a legitimate societal group outside of the "choice" they have made, which choice, to the Mormon mind, is *wrong.* They cannot be bigots if the group they seek to derail was *not* born to be who and what they are; if, however, they sought to derail a group that was *unable* to control the item uniting them – say, the skin pigment of blacks – they feel that then and only then could they be labeled as bigots.

Which they were, until 1978, when blacks were finally given the priesthood. (In other words, Mormons are no stranger to unintentional bigotry. If their faith dictates it, they will side with their faith and think themselves justified.)

I suppose at this point I could launch into the modern church's stance on blacks and the priesthood, but it's been done. Yes, Brigham Young and early church members (to my great horror, never having been made aware of the fact!) "owned" and abused people who John Taylor (another church president) actually called – *in the Journal of Discourses, which is considered scripture!!!* – niggers.[iv] (I apologize PROFUSELY for the use of that atrocious word here; I only use it to provide the same shock value it gave me, which is to recognize that a president of the church said it *and* called it *scripture.*) Suffice it to say that just about every Mormon under 60 was raised to think of blacks – and every other person with a differing nationality or skin tone – as *equals.* Not so with homosexuals…or with homosexual families.

*Pardon my tangent, but Mormons were really a thorn in the side of President Abraham Lincoln. He signed both the 1833 Morris Act prohibiting bigamy and polygamy, and the Emancipation Proclamation prohibiting slavery, in part to piss off the Mormons. I was *shocked* when I read some of Lincoln's quotes about the Mormons, and equally shocked to learn that the Mormons are the only religious group *ever* vilified (and rightly so!) in not one but *two* presidential inauguration speeches!

So much for Mormons being encouraged to recognize and uphold the law in the 12th Article of Faith! (All but the Morris Act and Emancipation Proclamation, I guess…)*

Back to homosexuality: when faced with the question, "Would I rather a baby be raised by two loving same-gender parents, or without any family in an orphanage?" the obvious answer (at least to me) has always been the former. *All* children *deserve* to be loved, to be taught to love, and to learn respect for others. One of my mother's very own cousins was the product of rape and was abandoned on the doorstep of an orphanage, where he lived his life to adulthood. He *never* felt loved, wanted, or valued until he created his own family in his early 30's, and even then he struggled desperately to make his family work, never having experienced family life himself. Ask the majority of active, devout members the above question, and I fear that, not being personally familiar with someone raised in an orphanage, their response might indeed be "orphanage."

Even believing that homosexuality was a choice, I still saw the value of raising a child in a family – of *any* sort – so long as they were well-loved and well-taught. Additionally, there are a considerable number of very well-adjusted now-adult children who were reared in families with two same-gender parents, just as there are a considerable number of truly wicked adults who were reared in families with two opposite-sex parents. I remember hearing the teenage son of a two-woman couple describe to a Senate Committee the love his family shared, and he proved himself a remarkable – and remarkably-raised – young man. Whoever you are, young man, your testimony helped to change at least one heart. Thank you. I still believe that the ideal is two opposite-sex parents, at least as far as learning to relate to individuals of each gender, but would never, *ever* begrudge a loving couple of any sort the opportunity to adopt a child in need of a family and bestow their love upon that sweet young soul.

Members (most especially in California) were asked to not only contribute their time to first Prop 22 and then, more intensely, Prop 8, but many were pulled into their bishop's office and asked to donate funds, as well. Some leaders even "suggested" an appropriate amount *based on the tithing receipts of that particular member*. When donation records were released (and anti-8ers began to threaten the lives, property, and general wellbeing of those who contributed), a friend and I perused the records because she was concerned that the $50 she and her husband donated might make her a target. It turned out that the donation records were made up of people who contributed much larger sums, some of whom were our current ward leaders or my childhood ward members. A family from my childhood ward had donated $10k, while three families from our current ward had each contributed $5k.

The Church asked, and they immediately obliged.

As though we don't already give enough.

In order to be considered temple worthy, you must freely give 10% of your *gross* income – including gifts, bonuses, etc – to the church each year, and attend "Tithing Settlement" at the end of the year to affirm to the bishop that you have, indeed, contributed the full 10%. Tithing money goes to Salt Lake City, ostensibly to pay the six-figure incomes of the general authorities, and to expand multi-million dollar Salt Lake shopping malls. (No joke. Former Church Office Building employees will attest to it, and independent estimates will tell you the church conservatively brings in between $4,000,000,000.00 and 6,000,000,000.00 each year. Yes, *billion*.)

But let's be a little more specific to the demands on *our* pocketbooks. We are required to pay:

- Tithing (10% of your gross income; goes to the general fund)
- Fast Offerings (a more generous version of the equivalent sum of the two meals your family sacrificed on Fast Sunday; distributed to

the needy on a local level)

We are occasionally asked to donate to or for:

- Friends of Scouting (contributions to the Boy Scouts of America)
- Building local temples
- Eagle Scout projects
- Young Women's Camp
- Various local service projects
- Mission funds for those serving missions locally and worldwide
- BYU's Perpetual Education Fund (and in our case, the BYU Alumni Association)

Above and beyond all that, the final covenant made with God in the temple endowment ceremony is the following: "...you do consecrate yourselves, your time, talents, and everything with which the Lord has blessed you, or with which he may bless you, to the Church of Jesus Christ of latter-day Saints, for the building up of the kingdom of God on the earth and for the establishment of Zion."

Consider the significance of that promise. We are *required* to give our *time*, our *talents*, and *everything we own* – AND *may someday own* – to *the church*.

But it gets even better: Part of the temple covenant includes the words, "And as Jesus Christ has laid down his life for the redemption of mankind, so we should covenant to sacrifice all that we possess, *even our own lives if necessary*, in sustaining and defending the Kingdom of God."

Yup. Everything you own, might someday own, and your life, too, while you're at it. Holy cow.

So when, like some of my more-mature peers during the construction of the Newport Beach Temple, you are called into the bishop's office and asked to donate thousands of dollars to the building of the temple so that local residents will have paid for it in its entirety without requiring money from the general fund, and the bishop explains that you are being asked to make this donation based on your tithing contributions (and, therefore, your estimated gross personal income), what do you do?

You give the church what it's asking for.

After all, you *already promised you would*.

Thanks to tithing records, the Mormon Church can easily estimate an individual or family's income; they need only multiply by 10. I have noticed, in the last few years, how many of the "big" callings in a ward go to wealthier individuals, likely because the ward leaders recognize those individuals as being "blessed." If they have been "blessed," they are clearly "righteous," right? A preposterously wealthy man we know, prior to moving out his 3,500 square foot home in our current ward and into a true mansion, held three rather significant callings...*at the same time.* Meanwhile, another man in our ward – one of the most profoundly intelligent and capable men we have ever known – has not been as lucky in business. He had no calling for many months, and only recently is serving in the capacity of teacher...for a primary class.

In our current ward, thanks in part to the economy, and in part to young people suffering a sort of self-entitlement mental illness, we have seen record numbers of foreclosures, short sales, and bankruptcy. It appears that, while our members are encouraged to pay their tithing, their mortgage obligations and other fiscal responsibilities are overlooked. I struggle with the idea that a family who purchased a home they could not afford are happily handed temple recommends so long as they pay their tithing, even though one of the temple recommend interview questions entails whether or not a person is "honest in their dealings with their fellow man." I fail to see how one particular family I know is considered "honest" enough to attend the temple: with two small children and another on the way, they are currently living in the home they bought at the height of the market for three times what it is now worth, and in the last 3 years have been "trying" to swing a short sale. They used those 3 years to redirect their mortgage payments – *which they can now make* – to the tens of thousands of dollars in credit card debt they owe, thanks to two new cars, ATVs, and other hobby-related "fun" items. Though they did, at one point, zero-balance their credit cards, they immediately purchased another $5k in various goods and are currently paying that down, piling the rest of their income into a savings account for whenever it is that the bank finally gets around to foreclosing on their 2800 square foot home.

Some college friends of ours took the cake with their "education" debt, racking up over $800,000.00 for a law degree, a psychology degree, and myriad trips around the globe (somehow financed into their student loans) because "they knew they'd never get the chance to travel after they had kids." They justified the sum by noting that "the prophet said that student debt is the only acceptable debt." Apparently a $10k trip to

Thailand was justifiable because they were, at the time, students. Needless to say, I find that profoundly troubling. (Note: As of last year, this couple has declared bankruptcy, but their student debt stands.)

Troubling, too, is the concept that we should pay tithing first, before we pay toward the financial obligations we assume. If you have to choose between paying rent and paying tithing, you are expected to pay tithing. The bishop will then help you make the rent. If you must choose between paying tithing or putting food on the table, you should pay tithing. The bishop will provide food from the "bishop's storehouse" to feed your family. (The storehouse is a sort of church-sponsored free grocery store containing food that church farms have grown, raised [in the case of meat], processed and/or canned, and distributed entirely via the volunteered time of the membership.)

Can we say *Nanny State?*

In many cases, had the individual used tithing toward rent or grocery bills, no one would have to provide anything. The person could then feel the self-esteem surge that comes from meeting financial obligations. We don't allow that, though; tithing comes first, taking care of yourself next. While we continue to preach and teach self-sufficiency, so long as you have given to the church, the church will take care of you, thus entrenching you in a state of dependency nearly impossible to separate from.

But you'll be taken care of.

Unless you work for the church, of course. A dear friend of mine worked for the church in their garment factory (literally making garments), and aside from rightly complaining about her meager pay (right around minimum wage), she told me all about the sweat shop conditions there, and about being let go when she had been away too many days thanks to nearly dying during the delivery of another Mormon baby. Though they won't take care of you when you work for them, at least they'll take care of you once they've fired you! (And is anyone else bothered by the "company store" bit there? The church pays you, and you give the church back 10% of what they just gave you. Eeek!)

What a phenomenal business model the church is when you think about it! With Disney-esque expertise, they maximize their income: they have a corner on the religious market called "Restoration." If they are the one and only true church, they own *the* supply...and outside of building temples and church buildings, creating that supply really doesn't cost much. (Especially when local members build their own temples and clean their own buildings.) All they have left to do is to generate demand. Enter the missionary force.

Let's walk through it:

- Start with a base of people who believe you – and only you – have what they need.
- Reinforce that idea with comprehensive books, bold but gentle speakers, and attractive people and buildings.
- Make sure the stakes for attaining the product are sufficiently high, but the product is free to "produce", invisible, and intangible: SALVATION.
- Demand those who seek to acquire your product spend 10% of their annual income to buy that salvation; those who pay less won't get a chance to glimpse the Emperor's New Clothes.
- Explain that delivery of your product is, for young men, contingent on their devoting two solid years of their youth to selling your product to new buyers, and tell them they must provide their own living expenses to engage in door-to-door sales for you. Be sure they explain the stakes involved in *not* aspiring to your product to ensure purchase.
- MAKE A KILLING IN YOUR BUSINESS DEAL.

The modern LDS Church has their business model down to a science. What I wouldn't give to think of a similar product!

*   *   *

In the historical church section, I touched on polygamy and misogyny in the early church, but such things still exist in the modern church today. This is not to say we are still polygamists; instead we know that, though we will not be required to accept another woman into our earthly families, we may very well be required to do so in the eternities. (I don't know a single LDS woman who *hasn't* contemplated the idea that she may, eons from now, be required to add a wife or two or ten to her marital relationship. Somehow we have learned to hate ourselves enough to be "okay" with that...or at least figure God will MAKE us okay with that...eventually.) As far as misogyny, though, it's visible all the time.

Take, for instance, what it's like to turn 12 in the modern-day church. As a 12 year-old boy, you are initiated into the Aaronic priesthood, involved in priesthood duties including the passing of the all-important sacrament, and expected to participate in the Boy Scouts, working toward becoming an Eagle Scout. You are taught that you will one day be in a leadership position in church, and that your introduction to the Deacons' quorum – the 12 and 13 year-old boys – is in preparation for that time.

As a girl, things are remarkably different. At 12, you are welcomed into the Young Women's organization as a Beehive and taught to remain virtuous so that one day a righteous returned-missionary priesthood holder can marry you in the temple. Everything you do is in preparation for becoming "a righteous wife and mother in Zion." (Here's hoping you don't have any other aspirations, because they aren't necessary.)

Though we have very little "power" in the church (and generally *want* very little power, whether because we're programmed not to care, or because it's just *more* responsibility we're not up for), there is ONE place where we are allowed to "hold the priesthood": the temple. Women have a very limited priesthood power during Washings and Anointings in order to bestow blessings, and only then because the men aren't allowed to be present with the woman receiving her ordinances. They have no choice: no matter how much the brethren may wish to be present, they will never be allowed in the women's changing areas.

Something occurred to me as I was writing about pornography earlier, and it seems to fit in best as a quick tangent in this area of modern church discussion: Maybe LDS men are so often porn addicts because they've been taught from their youth to devalue women. If the role and purpose of a woman is to breed and raise your children, and to care for you, your household, and your family, women exist entirely to serve your needs and keep you comfortable. What better way to have your "needs served" and to make you "comfortable" than to enjoy you for the very womanhood you offer? Why imagine you are capable of providing more? Women are of such little value intellectually and emotionally, it is more natural to appreciate their *physical* value. Enter pornography.

(Just a thought.)

Quick tangent: Joseph and Brigham clearly had no need for pornography, as they both had DOZENS of partners. No wonder it's tougher to abstain from pornography now!

I can think of no good segway from pornography to breeding in abundance, unless, of course, you count the obvious. Anyway: breeding and the modern church.

In this day and age, and particularly given the last few years' economy, my non-member peers are limiting their breeding. It makes sense: if you can't afford them, *don't have them*. Birth control is far cheaper in the long run. Additionally, if you can't *handle* them, don't have them. Yet Mormons do, in spades. This is for a few reasons, none of which is the church having taken a stand against birth control. That decision is left to husband and wife. Unfortunately, the church has managed to compromise both husband and wife, and Mormons continue to breed prolifically.

In the church, we are taught there was a preexistence, and that during the preexistence, we all lived in Heaven with our Heavenly Parents awaiting a human experience. According to the church there are a finite number of spirits in Heaven waiting for their turn, (odd; Heavenly Father must've stopped having sex with Heavenly Mothers!) and until and unless all those spirits have had a chance to experience human life, the Second Coming of Jesus Christ cannot occur. It is, therefore, our responsibility to give those spirits bodies. This facilitates two things: the ushering in of Armageddon and the Millennial Reign, and that those spirits will be born into strong Mormon families, raised in the true church to enjoy the restored gospel of Christ. (There is no mention of our duty to raise future tithe-payers. It's a given, and is a significant source of growth in both church membership and tithing since the church's inception.)

Those in the "green" community might shudder at the blatantly environmentally irresponsible breeding edicts passed down from Mormon to Mormon for the last two centuries, but Mormons don't worry about the environment; they worry about following the advice of church leadership, which is to bring not only converts, but babies into the fold. Further, Mormons don't believe there is any reason to be concerned with the environment, and their reasoning is twofold:

1. Global warming does not exist. (Mormons are notoriously socially conservative, and since it is generally liberals complaining about the environment, cognitive dissonance rears its ugly head and Mormons justify away the damage we are doing to our planet, particularly by mass-producing consumers.) D&C 104:17 says "For the earth is full, and there is enough and to spare…" We *can't*

use up the earth!

2. Even if global warming *did* exist, Christ will come again before we have a chance to destroy ourselves, at which point He will heal the planet and the earth will receive its paradisiacal glory. (In other words, Christ will save us; we needn't save the planet.)

So we breed and breed, whether or not we can afford the number of children we are breeding, and whether or not the planet can afford another flock of tiny consumers. It's all in the interest of doing as God commanded Adam and Eve in the Garden of Eden: Be fruitful, and multiply.

Though Mormon families are smaller today than they used to be – the average number of children had by member families these days is supposedly four, whereas it used to be closer to six – my LDS friends constantly complain that when they take their children to the grocery store or movie theater, what-have-you, they're constantly being asked "if all those children are really theirs." While my friends are offended by the question, I often imagine that the people asking are offended by the sight of a woman in a shopping center with her seriously ill-behaved brood, clearly unwilling or unable to control them. (Not all of them; some have exceptionally well-behaved kids, and those asking are just plain rude.)

While the size of Mormon families can prove problematic, (and not just from a fiscal standpoint; most eldest children in very large LDS families end up playing a huge part in raising their younger siblings, depriving them of some of the joys of their own childhood,) over-breeding and late breeding can and does lead to genetic issues and mentally and/or physically disabled children. I am personally familiar with at least 4 (Utah) families who "increased their flocks" to 8 and 10 children, the mother birthing her last child well over age 35, and sometimes into her mid-to-late 40s. In every single one of the above-noted 4 instances, the last child was born with Down's syndrome. (I have seen other disabilities crop up with last kids, too, but the chance that 4 families I know personally could conclude with babies affected with Down's speaks volumes for the chances that LDS parents take in the name of being fruitful and multiplying.)

Down's syndrome is no great tragedy – all humanity has value – *unless the condition was preventable*. In almost every case the husband and wife had been told that they needed to stop having kids, either because the mother was too old (read: "old eggs"), or because her health would suffer from another pregnancy. All 4 couples decided to "trust in the Lord" anyway, and each of their last children was born disabled. While I cringe at the thought, the church takes another position: reassurance.

You see, back in the preexistence, a war took place in Heaven (as outlined by Revelations) and Christ and two-thirds of the host of Heaven beat back Satan and his one-third, leaving Satan and his followers without the opportunity to lead human lives in human bodies. The remaining spirits followed Christ to await their turn to come to earth, but there were those who were particularly valiant in the war against Satan, and Satan decided, according to LDS doctrine, that it was important to really antagonize those particular earthly beings. In order to protect those most valiant souls from the influence and temptations of Satan, they were "blessed" with their disabilities, given the chance to have a body here on earth without the stress of being so sorely tempted to stray. In other words, a parent with a disabled child should be thankful that they were entrusted with the care of such a valiant soul, whose return to Heaven "in might and glory" has been made sure *by* their disability.

You cannot possibly imagine what a comfort that is to those families. That child will never flub up the possibility of an eternal inheritance because he or she cannot be held accountable for any of their personal actions or decisions.

The problem with that idea, outside of it giving parents free reign to make horrendously stupid breeding decisions, is that it negates the need for Christ's sacrifice to begin with! See, according to the church, the idea of the war in Heaven was a war of will: free will, offered by Christ, and forced decisions, offered by Satan. Christ said that He would follow God's plan, offering Himself as a Savior to mankind, but mankind would have the option to choose whether or not to return to God. Satan offered a different plan: he would make sure everyone returned to God upon their death by forcing them to live the way he wanted them to. They would never have the option *not* to return to God. No free will.

What about mentally disabled folk, then? If their disabilities prevent them from being mentally able to make choices, haven't they been denied free will? If God has ensured they will return to Him as a reward for their good choices before coming to earth, did He not follow the plan that Satan offered...the plan He found *unacceptable*? Did He Himself not remove their free will? Or did He just remove their accountability? Either way, free will is a farce, or Christ's sacrifice, unnecessary for a select few, becomes a farce.

But this logic is not followed in the LDS faith. After all, it's a *blessing* to be entrusted with the care of a once-valiant soul…one of the Noble and Great instead of the "Nachos."

Before you scratch your head: I took Sharing the Gospel as one of my religion classes at BYU. My professor, a very popular LDS speaker for teens and twenty-somethings, taught us one day all about the Noble and Great Ones and the "Nachos", or the "not-so" noble and great ones. He stated that during the war in Heaven there were those who were among the Noble and Great spirits fighting for souls on the side of Jesus, (we had no bodies; what kind of "war" was this, anyway?) those who were not so noble and great and who basically stood by and let the N&Gs do the fighting, and then there were those who fought on the side of Satan. (Note: according to early LDS doctrine, the absolute least-valiant during the War in Heaven were deposited into bodies with dark skin and denied the priesthood and blessings of the temple – meaning they could never reach the top of the Celestial Kingdom – as punishment for their preexistent ambivalence.) My professor implied that those who were born into the LDS faith were among the Noble and Great Ones, and proceeded to explain that "Where much is given, much is required," hence how imperative it was for us to serve missions and/or share the gospel with our non-member friends. We are NOBLE and GREAT, you see; it is our job, our duty, and our eternal responsibility to find those slightly-less-noble and slightly-less-great and bring them into the fold.

What do those ideas do to the mind of an 18 year-old Mormon kid? What could such a thing make you believe about yourself? About others? About other members?

This is what we in the modern church are raised to believe: we are *better*. We *know more*. We were *valiant* souls in Heaven, just not valiant enough to have been born with a mental disability. We…are…*SPECIAL*.

No wonder I've spent so stinking much of my life as a self-aggrandizing, self-involved pain in the ass.

Speaking of self-aggrandizing, just as I arrived at a point in life where I was attempting to develop myself and become a better person than the LDS faith could teach me to be, I found myself accepting a calling as the ward gospel doctrine teacher. This is a *big* calling, maybe not in importance, but in the time it takes to prepare a weekly lesson – I averaged 20 hours' study per lesson – and in the emotionally debilitating terror involved in attempting to teach up to 100 adults (ranging from 18-98) *anything* about the gospel. I served for an incredibly long period of time and thoroughly enjoyed teaching both the Old and New Testament, learning more than I ever could have imagined. True, teaching those books spawned a whole new set of questions about my faith, and the answers were dangerously much for my cognitive dissonance to handle, but I knew what I was teaching forward and backward. My lessons were well-received by some – most, even – but I very quickly developed a reputation in the ward as a self-aggrandizing know-it-all. (Apparently finding interesting and/or historical tidbits about the gospel to teach to the general membership is worthy of criticism and resentment. If the membership didn't know that Holy Land fig trees fruit before they flower and I had that tidbit to offer, I was considered a smarty-pants eager to intellectually show everyone up.) There were myriad complaints about me as a teacher, too, including that I should never have disclosed the idea that the woman with the issue of blood was likely suffering from uterine fibroid tumors, nor should I have mentioned menstruation, because those topics are inappropriate in a setting *where men might discover that women menstruate.*

Who knew? (None of the men present were supposed to have any idea that their wives menstruate…or likely where babies come from, for that matter…)

Amazing, the things we need to be protected from.

Amazing, too, the things we do to protect ourselves… emotionally, mentally, and physically.

Garments, I think I failed to mention, are the ultimate protection: we hear stories and rumors all the time of people who were in car accidents, construction accidents, fires, or who had other, similar experiences, and anywhere their garments rested, they were magically protected. I heard a story recently about a member serving in Iraq whose convoy was attacked, and everyone was massacred. When his body was discovered, his head and limbs had all been BURNED OFF, but the parts of his torso covered by garments were all healthy! (Of course, he was DEAD, so…even if the story IS true, what a lot of good that did him!)

So garments offer magical protection from bodily harm.

That said, I assure you, the only thing garments ever protected *me* from was my husband wanting to touch me. (More on that later.)

In the modern church, garments have changed over time (styles, fabrics, etc), the temple has changed over time (including now wearing garments under the bed sheet "shield" during washings and anointings and omitting the offensive suicide hand signals), and the Book of Mormon has changed over time (including, believe it or not, a promise made to the dark-skinned Lamanites that if they turned their hearts to the Lord, their skin would be made white; now the scriptures say that they will be made "pure," and skin tone is left out of it).

For a church that claims to have perfectly restored the fullness of the gospel of Christ, we sure do change with the times!

One thing that has not changed is the dedication of the modern church to the concept of free will. Since the devil's plan was to control us all, free will is considered our greatest blessing and our most basic human right. That said, we are duty-bound to use that free will to follow the commandments of God as outlined by His Church and His modern-day prophets, lest we be excluded from His presence in the hereafter.

As a child I loved the children's hymn "Follow the Prophet." These days I shudder when I hear even the chorus from the mouths of my very own babes:

"Follow the prophet, follow the prophet, follow the prophet, don't go astray. Follow the prophet, follow the prophet, follow the prophet, he knows the way!"

Incidents, Experiences, and Red Flags in My Own Life
and the Lives of Friends

I feel the need to fill this introduction with a million disclaimers, pleas, and explanations, but after careful consideration, I won't bother. Instead, I will be brief and to the point:

1. The incidents mentioned in this section may have entertainment value, but they are meant to illustrate my struggle, and the struggles of others, with the LDS faith.
2. Each incident I have either personally experienced, or have received direct from the source. They are true to the best of my knowledge and remembrance, though names and background details have been changed to protect those involved, whether they deserve it or not.
3. This section is *not* "fair and balanced" in its approach to the LDS faith, *nor is it intended to be*. Again, these are things that were "red flags" *for me*, and not meant to convey that they are typical of the LDS experience.
4. Rather than judge each incident (or those involved) individually, I ask that you reserve final judgment until the conclusion of the chapter, having read it in its entirety.
5. Additionally, please attempt to put yourself in my shoes as you read. Think of this section from the perspective of a woman whose thoughts, opinions, and feelings have been shaped entirely by a combination of the Mormon Church and the circumstances described here. Judge me as you will, but know that I have done and will continue to do my best to be the best person I can be, with the great hope that she will be better tomorrow than yesterday, and better ten years from now than ten years ago.

I present a ranting, mostly-chronological confessional, offering no apologies for presenting the world as I have experienced it.

Childhood

My childhood was relatively easy. My family is wonderful, we all got along (reasonably) well, and my folks, like I've mentioned, are normal...so other than wondering if I really should be baptized when I turned 8 (because I felt like it was expected, but I wasn't necessarily convinced), Mormonism didn't impact my childhood significantly.

I do remember a couple of friends on the playground telling me that Mormons weren't Christian, but I was so baffled when I realized not everyone went to our church, what they had to say didn't really register. *Not everyone worships like we do? You mean, some people DON'T sit for three hours every Sunday???* .... *Figures.*

Some things were Mormon-y, though: ever heard of Johnny Lingo? If you have, you're probably Mormon. Many years ago a story was written, and then a really corny musical followed, to relate the tale of Johnny Lingo and the 8 Cow Wife. (Or was it 10 cows?) The story was meant to convey that Johnny's wife, who utterly lacked both beauty and self-esteem, was the Ugly Duckling who grew up to be the Swan.

Johnny sought her hand, and he went above and beyond the norm, offering her father an 8 cow dowry. Most other women's dowries consisted of 1 or 2 cows. Everyone argued that the girl was not beautiful, had no special skills, talents, or intellect, and wasn't worth a pound of hamburger, but Johnny insisted, and his insistence made his new wife blossom. She only needed to feel her own worth to become someone amazing.

I loved this story as a kid – Johnny Lingo as a knight in shining armor – and wanted desperately to find a man who would offer my dad the proverbial 8 cows...until I learned of a quote from Heber C. Kimball referring to his own personal harem of wives as a herd of cattle, and realized that Johnny Lingo's wife shouldn't need a man to show her her intrinsic worth. She should instead develop herself as a person, recognizing the outcome of her own efforts as that which made her a worthwhile human being. The Johnny Lingo story was never the same again.

Johnny Lingo isn't the only Mormon propaganda movie. Since I was raised by converts, I did not grow up on Saturday's Warrior, Singles Ward, or The Best 2 Years. (My parents liked *real* movies.) It wasn't until I got to BYU that I experienced them, and they made me cringe even then.

Saturday's Warrior is a film about a family in turmoil, and part of it takes place in Heaven, where a childlike spirit is waiting her turn to inherit a body on earth as part of the subject family, but due to choices made by her family members, her opportunity to be born and raised Mormon is in danger of being revoked. Additionally, one of the children in the family gets involved in drugs and drinking (read: *gross and destructive sin*), everyone wears garish '80's clothes, and there is more singing, dancing, and bad acting in the film than in any I have ever seen…ever.

It's a Mormon classic.

Singles Ward, The RM, The Best 2 Years…all of these movies are made by Mormons, though not necessarily church-sponsored. Mormons love to believe that we have the exclusive ability to laugh at ourselves, and so LDS-oriented movie after movie is released in Utah to the delight of Mormon college kids, who love to be able to relate to what's onscreen, to laugh at silly husband-hunting women, and then return to our husband-hunting. The movies are painful to watch, and unless you're Mormon, you won't find them amusing or inspiring in the slightest. Don't bother.

Beyond propaganda, though, childhood was fun. As I got older, things weren't quite so fun. Aaaaaaand…here we go.

High School

In high school, knowing I would attend BYU, (yes, I was already that determined,) I selected my classes based on their ability to get me into BYU. Bible as Literature sounded Mormon-y, so I enrolled. We were told the first day of class that the NIV version of the Bible would be the preferred version for class, but since I already owned the King James version, I was granted permission to use my own Bible. Halfway through the semester-long class we had a test with an essay question about Cain's punishment for murdering his brother, Abel. In the Joseph Smith translation of the Bible, Cain is cursed with dark skin as part of his punishment, so when I answered the essay question, I was sure to include what was in my scriptures.

The very next day my teacher called me to her desk and asked what on earth I was talking about. "Cain was turned into a *black* man to *punish* him?" she disbelievingly demanded, the horror on her face (and in her voice) all too evident.

"Well, yes," I blurted. "Doesn't it say that in your scriptures?"

"*Does* it say that in *yours*?" She was clearly stunned.

I showed her my scriptures, including the offending verse, and she was doubly dumbfounded. "From now on you're going to use one of my spare NIV copies," she told me.

118

It was a miracle I passed the class.

Since boys occupy most of a high school girl's thoughts, though, let's talk boys: Mormons "can't" date until we turn 16...and even then, we're not supposed to focus on any one person. I dated a boy in my ward for a little while when I was 17, and we were on our way home from dinner one evening when we started talking about marriage and family. (Mormon, remember? It's all we think about.) He told me he wanted as many kids as the Lord saw fit to give him, and I told him that birth control and ejaculation would help to determine how many children that was. He argued he would never permit his wife to use birth control, no matter how many kids they ended up having, and I pointed out that that would not be healthy for either his wife or the family finances.

Mind you, a few weeks before one of the Young Women's leaders in our ward had told us all (with *great* pride) during a youth fireside – a Sunday evening get-together with a speaker and refreshments – that she and her husband had been so poor when they had their first child that "We lived off peanut butter and cereal for a year!"

"My wife will be sustained by the Lord," he told me, "and if having lots of kids means we have to follow Sister Youth Speaker's example and live off peanut butter and cereal, so be it."

"Then you're going to have to find yourself someone else to marry," I laughed, though serious.

He nodded. "Looks like I will."

That was our last date.

In high school I was infatuated with a childhood boy-friend, in great part because he was Mormon, and I imagined the two of us one day being wed. (It's like dreaming about a fairy tale marriage *all* the time!) He and I had been very close for many years, and at one point we sort of fell into making out with each other. Being that he was Mormon and so was I, our kissing never led to anything else, contrary to what generally happens.

In fact, our senior year in high school we went on a date, ended up making out in the back of my car for quite some time (thoroughly fogging the windows as a result), and about the time I finally got frisky (read: tried to get him to touch my chest over my clothing), he pulled back, shut me down, and explained that for some time he'd felt our making out was foolish and might eventually get us into trouble. He told me he thought it best for us not to kiss anymore – *at all, ever* – and that perhaps we shouldn't be going on dates together, if there was the potential for our date to conclude with inappropriate behavior. At exactly that moment the police knocked on my rear window and asked us to step out of the car, clearly thinking what was going on in the car was far different than what was *actually* occurring: my heart was breaking.

After the police sent us home (because we weren't doing anything wrong except parking in a parking lot where cars apparently couldn't park after dark), I dropped him off and cried the whole way home. We never did go on another date, never did make out even one more time, and from that day forward for years on end, he kept his physical distance from me. In fact, the only time after that I ever remember him even hugging me was after he came home from his mission. Six months later he was engaged to his wife, and they married soon after. It took me years to get over my devastation, and somewhere in the back of my mind, (until after he came home from his mission, even!) I was still hopeful we would be married someday...but deep down I knew I had blown it by not being righteous enough.

About the same time, my very dear friend (we'll call her Samantha) and I were discussing religion. I had shared the gospel with her, given her a Book of Mormon, and she even attended seminary with me, thoroughly interested for a time. Then she was handed some anti-Mormon literature, which was, in fact, really just "Mormon" literature, considering it contained only facts, journal entries, and early LDS documents of the sort that the modern-day LDS Church would love to forget.

She lost interest immediately – and rightly – and became a born-again Christian. A fellow teenage ward member of mine – remember Melissa the missionary? Same girl. Keep here in mind, because you'll be reading about her again in a moment – went with me to Samantha's church, and Samantha agreed, with her born-again friend Kelly, to attend ours.

Many awful things happened that day, all of which are embarrassing to recount but must be recounted, just the same. I could sort it all out for you, but I'd really just rather you felt an outsider's horror, imagining what all parties must have been feeling:

1. Melissa and I attended Samantha's church, and by the end of the hour-long meeting we were both in tears, distraught by how

committed these Christians were…*to the wrong faith.*

2. Samantha and Kelly attended our ward, and it was *fast Sunday.* Worse, a family in the ward who had been unable to have children had just adopted a newborn, intercepting the mother 6 months earlier on the very day she planned to have an abortion. The entire congregation wept as they took turns telling their tale.

3. After sacrament meeting, my friends were both in tears, distraught by how committed we Mormons were…*to the wrong faith.*

4. Also after sacrament meeting, one of the men in the ward saw Samantha and Kelly in tears and approached them, patting Samantha on the shoulder and telling her he knew why they were crying: *they had felt the Spirit.* He told them to hold on to that feeling, because it would someday lead them to the waters of baptism. Neither bothered to explain that that was *not* why they were crying.

5. Samantha and Kelly stuck around for Sunday school, and though I no longer remember the reasoning behind it, we all attended gospel doctrine that day. The topic was God. One of our ward members – an idiot in the extreme – felt the need to educate these young born-agains on the Truth about God, and expounded for fully 2 minutes on the location of His home: Kolob, a distant star, is next to the planet (name unknown) of the Heaven where God resides.

6. Samantha and Kelly did their best to control their giggles while Brother Idiot spoke, but Melissa and I were thoroughly destroyed, in part because Kolob was a "true principle" that was "meat, not milk," and should never have been brought up in the presence of non-members.

We all behaved abominably. None of us went into our exchange with the right spirit. But worst for me was Brother Idiot's account of Kolob, primarily because it was *true*: Mormons really do believe that the star next to the planet on which God lives is called Kolob. Melissa and I were loath to hear Brother Idiot mention it because it made us out to be the kooks we are. We are people who believe that God *dwells on another planet*, and He must therefore be, in the strictest sense of the word, an *alien.*

I never brought anyone to church with me after that.

No need to guess why.

Senior year concluded with a trip to BYU campus with Dad as sort of a "check it out" thing, and all went well...until the trip home. Keep in mind, I was raised to think of Las Vegas – which city I had slept through when we passed by on the way to Utah – as Sodom. Or maybe Gomorrah. I was sure whatever went on in Sodom and Gomorrah goes on in Vegas, so it really didn't matter which.

I had also had some (Mormon) family friends who moved to Vegas when I was just starting high school, and when they came to visit, they told us about how they had trained their children never to look at billboards around the city, which I assumed meant there were pictures of strippers and prostitutes displaying their wares on every corner. Vegas was a den of iniquity where bad Mormons went to elope and skip the blessings of the temple, where people lost their entire life savings in a single Satan-led bet, and where booze flowed freely through cigarette-laden air.

In short, I was truly, sincerely terrified of Las Vegas.

On the trip home I drove, my dad in the passenger seat, and as we drew close to Vegas, I started to shake...and get nauseous...and basically just totally freak out. In fact, I was so terrified of simply driving on the freeway through the city that I nearly smashed us into a freeway piling, and Dad had me pull off the freeway so he could take over.

By the time I had stopped the car – in the parking lot of a casino, mind you – I was shaking uncontrollably, (not only because I'd nearly killed us!) and I burst into tears, desperate to get away from the obscenity that was Las Vegas. I was afraid, I guess, that I might be infected by evil and...leave the church? (Ha.)

My dad was perplexed, of course, but then, he's never been a Crazy Indoctrinated Mormon Teenager about to graduate high school and leave the protection of home for the big, wide, scary (Las Vegas-style) world.

Frankly, my high school experience sucked...but not because I was Mormon. My college experience sucked, too, and that's ENTIRELY because I was Mormon, so on to BYU!

BYU

I attended BYU for four reasons:
1. They had my specific major, offered by only two other universities in the US.
2. The tithing fund subsidizes BYU, so tuition is cheap.

3. I was Mormon.
4. My ultimate goal in life was a temple marriage to a returned missionary, and BYU is a meat market.

I'm not kidding. BYU *is* a meat market. Most women who attend go there because on some level they want to utilize the school as a spouse locator and earn what we laughingly (but honestly) referr to as our "M.R.S. degrees." I spent freshman year in the dorms, and my very first week BYU held a start-of-school dance, so I went with some of the girls from my floor. It was at this dance that I realized in part the folly of my desperation for a husband, thanks to an introduction to NCMOs. NCMO, pronounced "nic-mo", since it is referred to by its acronym, means "non-committal make-out." Yes, there really is a term for enjoying a make-out session that likely will not end in marriage, and the very idea is a horror to some of the women I know, in and out of the church.

One woman I know (horrified by NCMOs) is incredibly proud of the fact that her very first kiss was on her wedding day. She still tells her children about her "VL" status, meaning, in LDS terms, she had "virgin lips." It wasn't until she and her husband had been married 15 years that she learned he had impregnated another woman while they were engaged, and that her husband's *actual* eldest child, the product of his cheating, was a few months older than *her* eldest child. (More on this later.)

I met a man at this first dance who was ever-so-much older and wiser than I; he was 23 to my 18, and though he wasn't necessarily my "type" as far as appearance goes, his attention, age, and status as a returned missionary made him so incredibly appealing that I was willing to not only overlook my decided lack of attraction, I was also willing to abandon my friends by accompanying him outside for a "chat" on a nearby bench. I was further willing to spend a solid two hours kissing him. We exchanged phone numbers afterward, and I left exactly two messages for him during the following two days.

He never called back.

He's not the only one. During the latter half of my freshman year I was sitting in a 2nd half New Testament class and caught the eye of a semi-attractive guy a couple rows over. I had to look again to ascertain the true level of his attractiveness – I remember giving him a 6 out of 10 – and when I saw him staring back, I looked away. After a moment I could not help myself and I looked back. He was still (or again) checking me out.

Please note, having grown up in California, I was accustomed to being checked out – and doing the checking out – quite regularly. Very little sex appeal is required in my home state to draw the interest or attention of the opposite sex. They are always willing to appreciate that which stands to be appreciated, bless their Californian hearts. Utah is completely different. When there is an endless supply of attractive and talented women desperate to marry, it is not necessary to give anyone a second look unless they happen to be a super model (and maybe not even then). All that is required to find the wife of your dreams is to pick the height, the weight, the hair and eye color, the home state, spirituality level, and preferred talents of your future spouse, match them to a passerby, and tell them God said you two were meant to be.

Done.

So my classmate was checking me out, and I wondered briefly if he might be a Californian. Turns out he was. He approached me after class, we exchanged phone numbers to set up a New Testament study date, and he called that afternoon. He picked me up at my dorm two days later and took me back to his apartment. When I walked in the door, one of his roommates introduced himself and said, "Oh, so you're the Three Glance Girl." I had been given a name. I felt special. I felt desirable. And after 90 minutes of discussing a few chapters of the New Testament, I felt immature and unstudied. We made out. He took me home. I never heard from him again, and he made sure, from that point forward, to enter class late and make a beeline for the door when class ended.

Upon reflection, "rating" him on a subjective scale of attractiveness was an obnoxious thing to do, but in my defense, I learned it from the boys in my freshman ward. I walked into my dorm one day – girls-only dorm, of course – and there were half a dozen boys from my ward hanging out in the lobby with my next door neighbor girls, both blonde, willowy, stereotypical southern Californians. I approached and was offered a chair. After sitting for a minute or two, I realized they were discussing the girls in our ward, or, more specifically, the bodies of those girls. When each girl was named, the boys took turns announcing the rating they would bestow upon that girl, based on her body type, shape, and size. The two girls I was with were given a 9 and 10 respectively, while I, 5' 7" and 114 pounds, was given a 7. (According to them, my breasts were small and my rear was large; otherwise I was "okay.")

This went on for a few minutes until they got to a girlfriend of mine who I happened to know had considerable health issues and had, as a result, an incredibly difficult time keeping slim. She was given a 2, and frankly, I was livid. In that moment it dawned on me that these idiots didn't know any of these women personally, and were unfairly judging us based on things most of us could not control. I finally told them they were full of crap and walked away...and then summarily gave my New Testament classmate a 6 a couple months later. I was as bad as they were, and I am still ashamed, though I'm sure *they've* forgotten all about it.

Freshman year presented other challenges where men were concerned: a friend of mine, who we'll call Rick, introduced me to his non-member best buddy "back home" in Arizona. We'll call him Randy. Randy and I became friends during his visit to BYU to see Rick, and we continued talking when he returned to Arizona, calling each other every couple days. I have always had a fascination with hypnosis, and he and I had discussed that at one point, but after a few weeks of talking, he asked about the possibility of a long-distance relationship and I declined, thanks to his not being LDS. He sent me an incredibly hateful email in response that threw me for a loop, and though I assume he was referencing my passing interest in hypnosis when he stated in his email that I had a "domination complex," what *I* got from reading the email was far more indicative of my mental state. I read the phrase as "*denom*ination complex," thinking he was referring to my religion.

When I replied, I explained that I knew Rick had told Randy that Mormons must marry Mormons, so he had *known* I had a "denomination complex". His answer was five words: "I wrote DOMINATION complex, dipshit." We never spoke again.

There was another boy, this one in my freshman ward, that I never spoke to again after a certain conversation. Let's call him Mitch. Mitch seemed like a really nice guy, and everyone thought he was incredibly good-looking, so I was eager to get to know him. On one of the nights we were allowed to visit the dorm rooms in the opposite sex dorms, I went to see him and tried to strike up a conversation. Note, *most initial conversations between Mormons of opposing genders involve each individual's desires and standards for a future spouse,* so when we chatted about what we sought in a husband or wife, it was *not* an unusual conversation. After I explained to Mitch what I was seeking, Mitch gave me his "short list", concluding with "…and she has to be a virgin." Now, at this point, I still was virginal, so though the idea did not personally offend *me*, I happened to know of at least two other truly amazing girls in my freshman ward who had lost their virginity and since repented. I challenged him on that point: "What if she's repented?"

"I don't care."

I was nonplussed. "But the prophet says that once you've repented, your sins have been washed away."

Mitch shrugged. "No hymen, no wedding ring. Let someone else have her."

Surely I had misheard. "But if the Lord has said that she's clean, shouldn't your standard be His?"

Mitch shrugged a second time. "There are plenty of other guys who could marry her. Like I said, *I'm* marrying a virgin."

I squinted at him. "Well, are *you* a virgin?"

He squinted back. "No. But *I* don't have to be. *She* does."

I literally threw my hands up. "Seriously? You're holding her to a standard you won't even hold yourself to?"

Mitch shrugged one last time; he actually might have shrugged a fourth time, too, but his next comment prompted me to leave the room without looking back, so I didn't see it. He said simply, "You've got that right." I did not reply directly, though I confess I'm fairly certain he heard me mutter "disgusting" under my breath as I walked out the door.

A friend of mine we'll call Beth also lived in the dorms our freshman year but worked in an off-campus apartment complex doing minimum wage housekeeping. Beth told me that a pipe broke one day and flooded the office basement, and that the apartment manager had called her in for Saturday overtime to help him clean it up. They worked almost an 8-hour day, and as they finished up, he offered to buy Beth lunch. She knew very little about him, but a meal is a meal, and so they walked to a local teriyaki bowl place, where they chatted over chicken and rice. About 15 minutes into the conversation Beth said he stopped dead, put his hand on hers, and told her that the Lord had made it clear to him that they were meant to be together, and he wanted her to seriously consider marrying him…as his second wife. Beth said she barely made it through the last 10 minutes of their shared meal, wolfing her food and promising to think about his proposal and get back to him. That Monday Beth quit her job…no surprise there. When your boss wants to bring you on board as wife number 2, you quit without a second thought.

Don't get me wrong, we all love sex, (Beth's boss certainly does!) but I think Mormons are a little more obsessed with it than most, and so the following incidents are all related to sex, and none of them are pleasant by any stretch. Feel free to skip ahead. If you choose to stick with me, however, I warn you: hang on tight.

My freshman year at BYU I went on a date with a "premie," another name for a man who has not yet served a mission. We had class together, and he seemed like a nice-enough guy. Dates with premies were always just for fun. They had missions to serve and wouldn't be marriageable for at least the next 2 years, so we never expected much from them. (That isn't to say they didn't expect much from us. Many sought a girlfriend who would "wait" for them, write them all during their mission, and then marry them shortly after they returned home. I had no desire to be one of those girls, and knew very few other girls who were willing to wait.)

We had a bite to eat, saw a movie at the Wilkinson Center movie theater, and then took a walk on campus to see what buildings were still open at 10 PM. Very near to the Wilk was the HFAC – the Harris Fine Arts Center – where we shared our class. We decided to browse the bowels of the building. The HFAC housed a number of theaters, the smallest of which was called the Nelke, and it had a stage on hydraulic lifts. We discovered we could get down below the stage so he could show me the hydraulics and how they worked, and once below, and after a couple minutes' exploration, he forced me into a corner and groped me relentlessly. At one point he shoved my hand inside his pants, and I began to cry, so he finally backed off.

The only person I told about the incident was a guy friend from my ward who we will call Joe. (Joe ultimately introduced me to my husband, interestingly enough.) Joe was LIVID. Ironically enough, Joe served a mission in the *very same place and district* as my date, and immediately went to his mission president to report the other elder's pre-mission behavior. The elder remained in the mission and to my knowledge (and Joe's) went unpunished by the mission president. He did not go unpunished by Joe, however, who told everyone in the mission about how Elder Molester had molested his friend back at BYU, bless Joe's heart.

A couple months later I had a similar experience. I had been making out with Joe's roommate (quite the BYU pastime); we'll call him John. John had a girlfriend back home, but seemed okay with spending copious amounts of time with me, and as I grew very quickly attached, we began regular make-out sessions. Eventually they led to what everyone else would consider some very tame friskiness, but it was enough that, aside from pissing off his girlfriend had she known, he probably would have had to delay his mission a few weeks for repentance's sake. (He ultimately *did* have to delay his mission – by a few *months* – but not because of me.) Because he had a girlfriend, I felt perfectly comfortable going on dates myself, as I had with Molester Man from class.

One of my other dates was with my Film TA, a 25 year-old RM who promised to introduce me to a few awesome flicks. He took me to dinner, then to a video store, where he asked me to hang on his arm for the sake of the store owner, a friend of his. I did so, enjoying the attention. He picked a movie and we went back to his place, an off-campus house rented by him and three other roommates. We started the movie, and about 15 minutes in, he disappeared into the kitchen, returning with a bottle of wine. He offered me a swig, and when I declined, he *drank the entire bottle.*

To that point I had *never* been around *anyone* who was drinking. That may be incredibly hard to believe, being that I was 18 and attended high school in southern California, but it's the truth. Though I attended high school dances and associated with people who were clearly drunk (and stank to high heaven to prove my theory), I had never actually *seen* anyone drink. I was floored...and scared. (Seems silly, I know, but again...*Mormon girl.*)

By the time he had finished the bottle (about ¾ of the way through the movie), he had begun to rub my shoulders. I wasn't sure whether to let him – it felt nice, no doubt about it – or to tell him to lay off, so I squirmed a few times and then tried to ignore him, but he refused to be ignored. He turned me sideways on the couch, and I noticed that at some point while I'd been watching the movie, he had unzipped his pants. Worse, and it absolutely scarred me to see it, his penis was erect and protruding through the slit in the front of his garments. (Men's garment pants look like knee-length, white versions of men's boxer-briefs, complete with front opening.)

Even as I tried to stand, he shoved me back down onto the couch, climbed on top of me, pressing me flat and pinning my arms, and orally raped me *through* his "sacred" garments. I gagged and vomited on him, and he pointed me to the bathroom to clean myself up. Reentering the room, I found him wearing a fresh pair of pants and holding his keys. He was ready to take me home.

Not having had any experience with alcohol to that point, I was terrified of his being behind the wheel, but it was before the days of "everyone-owns-a-cell-phone" and I could not call anyone to come get me, nor did I have any clue where I was to tell someone where to find me. He climbed behind the wheel and I sat in the front seat, hanging on for dear life (though mildly amazed at how well he was driving). He sang Christmas carols all the way back to the dorm, actually tried to kiss me goodnight, and I headed inside, where I summarily threw up twice more (once in the shower) just thinking about the experience. My roommate, with whom I did not get along, noticed something was off and asked about it, but when I declined to comment and stated instead that I was going to go shower, she said "FINE" and left me alone.

It was two months before I could bring myself to tell anyone about it, and when I did, my friends assured me that I needed to go to my bishop and report the offense. I waited another month, and then one of my friends came to me to let me know that *she* had reported it to the bishop, and the bishop wanted to talk to me personally. This bishop and I had had a run-in once before, which I will discuss in detail later on, but which kept me from wanting to share my tale of woe with him. Discovering that someone had talked to him without my knowledge was a horror.

I did not hear from the bishop for some time, however, until two weeks before the end of my freshman year, when the ward's executive secretary called to inform me that the bishop wanted to meet with me. I went in two days later and sat across the desk from the bishop, waiting for him to start the conversation. "I hear you have something to tell me about one of the male students here at BYU," he began. I confirmed that that was the case, but told him that I knew he'd already been made aware of the situation. He asked me to give him "my version" of events, so I offered a brief summary, wanting to get through it as quickly as possible.

"So you mean to tell me that you were in this young returned missionary's apartment all alone with him? And what time did you say this alleged event took place?" I explained that he had indeed taken me to his home, and that I wasn't sure if we were alone because I never saw his roommates, but that we had stayed in the living room the whole time and I was back to my dorm before midnight, the BYU curfew for members of the opposite sex to be out of one another's BYU-approved housing units. (Having a boy in your apartment 15 minutes past midnight is enough to get you thrown out of BYU housing – maybe even thrown out of BYU – regardless of the reasoning behind it.)

This was when he dropped the bomb: "I'm sure you're aware by now that John [Joe's roommate] had to postpone his mission, and I was advised by his bishop that *you* were to blame. I have to admit, considering your behavior with John, it's incredibly difficult for me to believe that a *returned missionary* – and a *TA employed by BYU* – would engage in such activities. I don't think you're being honest with me. Furthermore, I think you're trying to cover up your own sins by foisting them onto someone else."

You can only imagine how stunned I was. To this day I lack words to describe it.

"So here's what we're going to do," he continued. "You're going to write me a letter. You're going to write a letter no fewer than four pages long, and have it to me by Friday. [It was Wednesday.] In that letter, you'll explain to me why I should allow you to stay at BYU…why I should let you keep your place as a student here when there are thousands of righteous young men and women who would kill for your spot. You're going to lay out your sins for me, and demonstrate the depth of your penitence. Once I've had a chance to read through it a few times, I'll get back to you on whether or not I'll be signing your ecclesiastical endorsement, but if I were you, I wouldn't plan on being back next Fall."

Ultimately I dried my own tears, booted up my computer, and spent all night writing a five page letter to my bishop confessing my myriad sins, taking full responsibility for John's mission delay and for "seducing" my TA, and then pleading desperately to be able to remain at BYU, stating that I was relying on the mercy of the Lord and His representative here on earth, my Bishop, who I trusted entirely to perform the Lord's will in regard to the fate of my educational goals. I delivered it to the bishop in a sealed envelope with tears in my eyes (and no small amount of outrage and bitterness in my heart), and a week later he called me with the news that he had signed my ecclesiastical endorsement, convinced by the outpouring of my soul onto paper that I was truly contrite.

I gagged on my drunken Film TA's penis, forced into my mouth through the hole in the front of his garments, vomited on us both, and prayed fervently all the way home that my drunk driver would deliver my 18 year-old self safely to my dorm… *then apologized for it to my bishop.*

Welcome to Hell.

But I am *nowhere close* to the only one. A roommate came home one evening from a blind date, looking wild and crazy, with the strangest smile I'd ever seen on a woman's face. I asked how her date went. She said it was interesting, and laughed. I followed her lead and laughed too, asking if she'd "gotten any," as in, participated in the notorious NCMO. She laughed again and said, "Oh, yeah, you could definitely say that," and then she retreated to the living room, and I headed to bed. When I awoke the next morning she was seated on the couch with one of our roommates (where she had stayed all night long), not moving, not speaking, only staring straight ahead. It turned out she had been date-raped.

Of course I had no idea, but to this day all I can think is, "My GOD, why did I have to greet her with THAT?" I don't know that I will ever overcome the guilt and shame associated with asking whether or not she had "gotten any." I can only hope she understands.

Speaking of rape, there is a pathway through campus leading to off-campus housing that heads down a very large, very steep hill. Due to the number of rapes committed in the area, it has earned the nickname "Rape Hill," and co-eds are warned never to take the Rape Hill path alone after dark. Though there is no published total of the number of rapes that have taken place there (that I know of), the idea that there have been enough to designate part of BYU's "dedicated" (read: blessed by a general authority with priesthood power) campus as "Rape Hill" makes me ill.

Another friend did not attend BYU. She was raped instead by her bishop's returned-missionary son at 16. After reporting the incident to her parents, they discussed the issue with their bishop, his father. Ultimately both the bishop and her parents decided not to report the rape to police, concerned by the amount of legal and psychological "harm" that might come to him if police found out. Apparently no one was concerned about the harm that came to my friend when even her parents, the people she was supposed to be able to trust above everyone else, decided against pressing charges. 2 decades later, she still sees a therapist…and is still a member.

I grew up with an LDS family (in our stake) that had quite a few children, and became friends with one of their daughters, a couple years older than me, when we both attended BYU. It was then that she told me about the remains inside her family's skeleton closet: as a youth, she was raped by her younger brother. About that same time her older brother persuaded her *much* younger sister to fellate him, offering candy as her incentive. (Note: She is the *second* Mormon girl I've known who was persuaded to fellate on a family member for candy and/or spare change.) My friend eventually told her mother, who instantly sided with her sons and denied anything had happened. She and her little sister went instead to their bishop, who also swept the incident under the rug. In despair, and at age 24, my friend finally left the church. I have lost track of her, but I pray for her well-being and for the well-being of her little sister.

A very dear friend was raped at 19 by a local real estate returned-missionary big-wig in Utah County a few years back. He was married with children, and her boss at the time. He had only one other employee – his female office manager – and my friend (we'll call her Ann) was sort of a gopher for the real estate guru and his office manager. The office manager left on vacation shortly before Christmas that year, leaving Ann and the realtor to wrap things up in the few days left before Christmas. On her last working day before a week's vacation, Ann was combing through documents on a desk in the small house that served as the realtor's office when he approached and struck up a conversation that turned quickly inappropriate. She grabbed a stack of mail and excused herself, intending to run to the post office to end the conversation, when he grabbed her. For the next two hours he raped her orally, anally, and vaginally, with his tongue, penis, and a knife, severely scarring her vaginal canal and damaging Ann's left nipple so badly that she was unable to breastfeed from that breast. He chased her around the house, beating down doors when she managed to temporarily escape to rooms with locks, and punished her for trying to escape him by carving her up with his knife.

After two solid hours Ann escaped from the house, running naked into the street and driving home through the snow, covered only by the sweater she had left on the front seat of her car. She pressed charges and he spent six months in jail, during which time his wife and children left him. He is now free, and lives exactly four houses away from *another* dear friend of mine (we'll call her Janet), who reports that he is regularly seen bringing home strange women. On one particular occasion Janet was out for an early-morning run and happened to be passing his house on her way home. He came out the front door, dressed only in pajama bottoms, and Janet said that in the doorway of his house was an overly made-up woman wearing the pajama top, and *only* the top. Janet told me he reached for the newspaper on his lawn, and then yelled (at 5 AM) to the surrounding neighborhood, "Yup! Here we are! Everybody stare at the sinner fetching the paper! Come one, come all, the sinners are out in the open!" Janet looked around, saw no one around but she herself, rolled her eyes, and headed home.

Though far less dramatic than Ann's experience, I dated a returned-missionary while still at BYU who I believed I would end up marrying. Let's call him Frank. Though my attraction to Frank waned when he stopped working out (and consequently put on a tremendous amount of weight very quickly), I was certain that *this* was the man the Lord had given me to marry, and I would just need to adjust to his stupid sense of humor and 60-pound weight gain. We dated for 9 months, during which time three odd things happened:

1. Someone in his apartment spent over $500 on phone sex.
2. He kept me, with great anger and gusto, from putting away a few pair of folded socks in his closet drawers.
3. We went to a concert (where I got my first-last-only contact high from copious amounts of marijuana smoke), returned to his house where I slept off the drugs, and then he took me home, behaving very strangely toward me.

I had one semester left at BYU before graduation, during which time I finished my student teaching, at one point accompanying a large group of teenagers to a convention in Cedar City. Frank made arrangements with my supervising teacher to meet the group in Cedar City as a chaperone. During our off-hours the second day of the field trip, he pulled me away, complaining that I seemed distracted and he wanted some time to have me to himself. I obliged and we hopped in the car. He drove for some time and I lost track of where we were, until suddenly we were in the middle of nowhere. He stopped the car and began to yell, at which point I tried opening my door. He had engaged the child locks. I was stuck. He calmed down, then transitioned to sobbing. (Note: Frank's father committed suicide when Frank was 13, and he has a family history of emotional instability, including a schizophrenic sister. I had good reason to worry.)

Frank proceeded to use me as his confessional, admitting that the $500 phone sex bill was his. He also explained that, back when I had tried to open his closet door to put away his clean socks, he had flown angrily across the room to stop me because he had a floor-to-ceiling stack of porn magazines in his closet, part of a collection of pornography to feed his masturbation obsession. Finally, Frank confessed that while I had been sound asleep on his couch sleeping off my concert contact high, he had repeatedly molested me. (Believe it or not, I'm a sound-enough sleeper, and sensitive enough to medications, it doesn't surprise me he was able to accomplish such a thing without my being aware.)

Frank explained that he knew that God wouldn't *let* me love him, and he was sure I had been distant the last couple days because God had prevented me from desiring to be affectionate with his sinful self. He had decided he just couldn't live with himself anymore, and since he couldn't live without me, either, *but God wouldn't let me be with him*, he was now completely at a loss.

I changed in an instant.

I went from horrified and sickened to assuming a completely false calm and compassion for him, holding him in my arms (even as I shuddered at the thought) and letting him weep on my bosom. I told him I was distracted, not because I didn't love him, but because I wanted to prove myself to the teacher I was teaching under, and because I felt a grave responsibility for the few dozen teens in my charge. Furthermore, I loved him very much, but with three months 'til my education was complete, I had done a poor job showing it, and I apologized profusely. I told him I forgave him, that I didn't think pornography was a big deal, that I looked forward to marrying him (five months from then; he planned to propose right after I graduated, and we supposed we'd be married two months after that) so his future phone sex would be free. I also told him I understood the temptation he suffered, seeing me lying drugged on his couch, and didn't blame him for touching me. I then proved my love by kissing him. Repeatedly. *And I managed not to throw up.*

Sufficiently comforted, he took me back into town, we had lunch, and then returned to chaperone the students. I spent the following two days pretending to be utterly smitten, putting on an Oscar-worthy performance. By the time I returned to BYU I was *done*. I would not return his calls or answer his emails, and finally a male friend picked up the phone when he called and told him to get over me; my friend and I were now a couple and Frank was out of the picture.

Frank tried once more when I returned home temporarily after graduation, showing up at my folks' house while I was gone and staying two full hours to await my return, chatting with my parents all the while. I saw his car in the driveway when I arrived home, but kept driving. I stayed out four more hours, just to be sure he'd be gone by the time I came back. My parents told me I'd missed him and advocated emailing him to formally break things off, which I did. Frank replied with a viciously angry email, then a repentant email, and finally a very cold sayonara.

I was glad to be well-shot of him, you can imagine.

One of the most atrocious sex-related things I've heard of, as though my friend's being raped with a knife wasn't enough, was the suicide of a former student from the Salt Lake area. At 18 he was preparing for a mission, something expected (back then) of every 19 year-old boy in the church. (It's still expected, of course; now it's just expected of every *18* year-old boy.)

It happened, however, that in high school this young man had fallen in love, and he and his girlfriend, as do so many other teens, had sex. Since his father was bishop of his ward, he hadn't felt comfortable going to his dad to repent, and instead lied his way through his mission interviews.

His guilt – both from having sinned, and from having lied about his worthiness – was so intense, the day after his mission call came in the mail, he hooked up some tubing to the tailpipe of his car and killed himself. His suicide note was on the front seat, stating he would rather go straight to the Telestial Kingdom (the lowest of the three levels of Heaven where Mormons believe suicides go) as a suicide than face himself in the mirror as a sinner and a liar even one more day.

This was the very same kid who, when I had been sick for an extended period while teaching, got together with two other kids in his class and they all brought me sunflowers the day I came back. He had a really big heart, this boy, which heart was broken by the weight of expectations placed on him by his church, his family, and his testimony of the "truth" of the gospel. (Knowing what I do now, imagine how sick this makes me...)

Another friend of mine from freshman year at the Y sought a unique way of getting out of his mission, too: he lost his virginity...to a *man*. This kid came from an extremely wealthy family from the Salt Lake establishment and had been promised the car of his choice – in his case, a BMW – if he served a successful mission.

While eager for a brand new car, he was also eager to get on with his education, and wasn't sure if he wanted to bother with a mission, even at the expense of a BMW. He wanted the option to come home from his mission should he decide he hated it, and sought out a homosexual for sex. (He is absolutely, totally 100% straight. I realize his having sex with a man makes that debatable by default, but the reality is he is in no way attracted to men.) This was his "anti-mission insurance," he called it; if his mission sucked as badly as he anticipated, he could then go to his mission president, confess that he had "dabbled" in homosexuality, and he would immediately be sent home.

Why he bothered pursuing as a sexual partner someone to whom he could never be attracted, at the same time exposing himself to whatever diseases the man might have been carrying when he could have protected his crotch *and just lied*, I'll never know. And it turned out that it really didn't matter anyway. He was called to a foreign mission, had a rollicking good time with a companion who also had no desire to serve a mission, and learned a new language and a new way of living. He ultimately finished his mission, got his BMW, and moved abroad on his parents' dime, leaving the church and shacking up with woman after woman after woman.

At least he had "gay insurance" tucked in his back pocket!

In direct contrast: aaah, the *innocence* of (some) Mormons. My sophomore year at BYU, we had one of the sweetest, gentlest, quietest men in the world as first counselor in the bishopric. One Sunday he was conducting sacrament meeting, and from behind the pulpit, he described making a recent mistake as having "pulled a giant boner." I and three friends did *everything* in our power to prevent ourselves from laughing uproariously, including pinching each other...*hard*.

When we realized that we were the *only* people in the entire congregation who caught the gaff, or rather, we were the only members who even realized there *had been* a gaff, I had to excuse myself to the bathroom to laugh myself to tears. When I related the story to my parents, they told me their former bishop, a police officer, had, during a talk, mentioned women forced to walk the streets of loneliness, proclaiming that it was our duty to love them. His phraseology left something to be desired: He said all he wanted was to love those street-walking women. Mom, too, had had to excuse herself when she dissolved into laughter.

On the subject of Mormon innocence, I remember walking into a neighboring apartment at BYU seeking eggs; we were out, and I needed one for a recipe. The four girls in the living room ushered me in, produced an egg, and asked me to solve a puzzle, imagining for some reason I would have the answer to their question. I braced myself. You never know what a bunch of young Utah Mormon women will come up with.

I was right to brace myself: "What's oral sex?" they asked.

Frankly, I couldn't imagine there was room for debate. "Um…what do you guys think it is?"

One daring soul spoke up. "Actually, we're arguing about whether it's phone sex, or French kissing."

I couldn't help the disbelieving snort of laughter that shot from my nasal passages. "Really?"

Another offered, "I think its phone sex. You know, having sex *orally*. With your *voice*."

The first chimed back in. "I think its French kissing, because his tongue goes in your mouth, kinda like…well, you know…*real* sex. Only with his *tongue*." [I guess a woman using *her* tongue is off limits…]

I must have stood there looking dumb for a minute or two, because one of them finally brought me back to myself. "So, which is it?"

I looked from girl to girl and shrugged. "None of the above, and that's all I'm saying. Go get yourselves a sex textbook or something. You've all got a lot to learn if you're ever going to keep your future husbands happy."

Hey, at least I got my egg.

Sex has played into some incredibly awkward moments in my own Mormon life, and the following three instances may prove to embarrass me more than any others listed herein. Please don't judge me too harshly; I promise it could never match how harshly I've had to judge myself.

Junior year at BYU a very good friend and roommate got married. I was her maid of honor. I could not attend their temple wedding, of course, not having been through the temple myself, but I did what I could to participate, and she and I flew to her home state, where the wedding would be performed. On the flight we talked about the upcoming wedding, and almost nothing else. She admitted that she had visited the gynecologist about a month prior for her birth control, but (at 20) she had never had a gynecological visit before, and had never used a tampon for fear of "ruining things for her future husband." Her gynecologist warned her she was exceptionally tight, and gave her some spacers of increasing size to use to stretch herself out enough to accommodate her husband, warning that if she chose not to follow her doctor's advice, sex would be incredibly painful, if not impossible. I asked if she had done as the doctor ordered, and she assured me that "she could never!"

"Besides," she told me, "the Lord knows I've done everything I can to wait for marriage. I'm sure He'll take care of things for our wedding night."

I pointed out that she had gone to the doctor to be advised about how to prepare for her wedding night, and choosing not to follow doctor's orders was a bit like turning down the Imitrex she used for her migraines because "God would understand her desire for the migraine to go away and rid her of it, her dedication to getting rid of it evidenced by her having simply visited the doctor." If the doctor had a pill – or in her case, spacers – to prescribe, wasn't it in her best interest to do as directed?

"I'm sure I'll be fine," she said, rolling her eyes.

Enter Stupid Me. At the wedding reception I cornered her new husband, pulling him aside for just a minute to ask him to "go easy on his new wife." I understood from personal experience just how painful a woman's losing her virginity could be, and imagined it would be infinitely more difficult for my friend, thanks to her doctor's warning and her refusal to accept the doctor's "prescription". I stuck my nose in, wanting to prevent her from experiencing substantial discomfort even though it wasn't my place, and *actually tried to tell her now-husband how to have sex with his wife* (ie. "go easy").

He told me that it was none of my damned business, it was between him and her, and they would take care of it. He was right, of course, and I was being self-righteous. It dawned on me immediately and I apologized, excusing myself to the bathroom for a good "OhgodIfeelsostupid" cry.

Incidentally, it was three weeks before they were finally able to have sex, and it was agonizing for her. They had sex exactly twice in the first six months of their marriage until she went to her gynecologist for advice that *this time* she promised to follow.

The point is, the self-righteousness ingrained in me by my LDS upbringing reared its ugly head, and the stupidity ingrained in my friend by her LDS upbringing did the same, humiliating me and mortifying her.

I was a self-righteous idiot my senior year, too, when my roommate we'll call Leah, who I loved dearly, moved away from our complex. I discovered a few months later that she had moved in with her boyfriend in Salt Lake, and was gripped by some sort of horrifyingly self-righteous indignance. I borrowed another friend's car and headed straight up to Salt Lake "to visit," spending the first five minutes catching up, and the next hour berating her for her stupidity. I also noted that moving in with her boyfriend was "grounds for excommunication", and told her she was "playing with fire."

She never spoke to me again. *I don't blame her.*

This next incident will probably humiliate me more than anything else in this entire book. I share it with you not out of a desire for self-flagellation, but because it illustrates the depth of the insanity that is part and parcel to Mormondom. Please note, I discovered in college that I *like* sex. (I know that's an incredibly shocking statement – I mean, really, who likes *sex?* – but there it is.)

I did indeed have sex before I was married (more shocking still!), and at one point, I briefly dated a guy from out of state whose family had moved to Utah upon their conversion to Mormonism. He was a couple years older than I was, and we had met at a dance club in Salt Lake and hit it off. After dating for a few weeks, we became intimate.

Directly after our one-and-only sexual experience, however, he broke down in tears, telling me he felt like his grandmother, who had passed away only a few months before, was looking down on him from Heaven with great disapproval. Also, she had not converted to Mormonism prior to her death, so he wasn't even sure she was *in* Heaven.

I felt like someone had dropped an anvil on my chest. Here I was, a BYU girl, having sex with a relatively new convert who had just lost his beloved grandmother, and he was "more sensitive" to the "spirit" than I. So, with a huge dose of overwhelming resignation, I sat down with him and told him the following: "Look. You're worried about your grandma; I get it. I'm going to give you a quick rundown on the plan of salvation, okay? You probably won't feel anything when I tell you about it, considering I'm about the least-worthy person possible to try to tell you any of this, but you need to know that Grandma is okay, and I'd love to reassure you."

We got dressed, sat down at the kitchen table, and I mapped out for him the plan of salvation, explained baptisms and temple work for the dead, and assured him Grandma was *just fine*. He cried a little more, took me home, and before he left we broke things off, the feeling mutual. I have no clue what became of him, but upon reflection, and rather than breaking the entire experience down to try to wade through the insanity behind it, I'll just say that there was not one fiber of that experience – participants included – that wasn't totally, completely, and royally fucked up. I cannot possibly explain, nor do I believe I need to, the degree to which I am thankful for having finally decided to leave the church.

Shifting gears for a few pages...let's discuss modesty. What is the standard for a Mormon girl? I know I mentioned it earlier, but I think it bears restating. (I don't care much about the standard for a Mormon guy. Aside from not wearing tank tops, there are very few male styles that men in the church are unable to sport.) Mormon women are expected to cover everything garments would cover. This means all skirts and shorts must be knee-length or longer, and should not rise above kneecaps when seated. Shoulders must be covered by (at the very least) cap sleeves, and fabric must cover the belly, the swell of a bosom, and the whole of your back, ruling out tube tops, strapless tops, spaghetti strap tops, tank tops, shells, and anything backless, midriff-baring, low-cut, or translucent in any area where skin should not be seen (as in, no long-sleeved tops with sheer sleeves). Swimsuits must be one-piece, and clothes should never be "too" tight. Additionally, for Sunday dress, I've seen many a Young Women's leader have a minor tantrum because one of the young women wore flip-flops to church.

This is all fine and dandy, but I confess it makes it incredibly difficult to buy clothing. (Many of the Mormon women I know invest in tunic-length, bosom-hiding, MLM-hawked camisoles to wear underneath short-sleeved tops on the off chance that if they bend over, their back and/or belly skin won't be exposed.)

More importantly, it has a horrendous effect on men in the church. Howso? A non-member woman wearing *any* type of the aforementioned clothing becomes a sex object. Worse, a woman inside the church wearing anything "immodest" skips right on past "sex object" and makes the jump straight to "whore". (After all, "she knows better.") It encourages judgment from the men, and immediately makes a shoulder, a belly button, or any amount of visible thigh something profoundly naughty.

It is *substantially* worse at BYU. A male friend of mine, also from southern California, attended BYU at the same time I did. He went from spending hours at the beach with our bikini-clad non-member CA friends to adopting the BYU modesty ideal. When we returned home from freshman year for summer break, a group of us headed to the beach, same as always, but this time my friend suffered needlessly, thanks to the expectations implanted in his brain by his BYU experience. He could not have a conversation with any of our female friends without staring at her breasts, and spent the entire day fighting a series of erections.

In other words, BYU's insane emphasis on modesty convinces men that immodest women seek after something other than fashion, and it turns knee caps and shoulders into erection fodder. A perfect example of this occurred in February 2012. A young woman at BYU was approached by a male stranger, who handed her a slip of paper. Being Valentine's Day, she imagined it would be something sweet. Instead, the note read: "You may want to consider that what you're wearing has a negative effect on men (and women) around you. Many people come to this university because they feel safe, morally as well as physically, here. They expect others to abide by the Honor Code that we all agreed on. Please consider your commitment to the Honor Code (which you agreed to) when dressing each day. Thank you."

If you google "BYU girl modesty note" you'll find both a photo of the note, and a photo the girl took with her camera phone of herself a couple minutes later in a bathroom, showing exactly what she's wearing: a tunic-length baby doll dress with leggings and knee-length boots and a long-sleeved sweater. (It was February, after all.) I would struggle to find a more modestly-dressed person *anywhere*. Clearly, the man who wrote the note has some serious BYU-generated issues, or, more accurately, Mormon-generated issues. His words are not those of every Mormon kid on BYU campus, of course, but my point is that this incident is indicative of the general attitude of Mormons, BYU students in particular.

I remember attending a dance at BYU and wearing a sleeveless ball gown covered by a woven-style bolero jacket that was slightly sheer but went perfectly with my dress, turning it into a short-sleeve gown. When I arrived at the dance with my date, I was told that because the matching cover-up I'd spent weeks searching for (and what was, to me, a substantial sum of money to purchase) was sheer enough that the *outline of my dress top could be discerned*, I was required to wear my date's jacket the entire time I was there, or I would be asked to leave.

I put on his jacket, and two hours later was sweating badly, so I took it off to cool down for a few minutes. One of the BYU Honor Code representatives at the dance immediately approached me and my date, explained that she knew I had been told to wear my date's jacket because my attire was immodest and inappropriate, and asked us to leave. We declined, explaining that I was overheating and would shortly replace his coat, and she nodded.

She returned less than a minute later with two male colleagues. The three of them escorted us to the door, kicking us out of the dance. We were not permitted reentry, whether I wore his jacket or not, and no amount of pleading or pointing out that we had spent $75 to purchase our tickets would sway them. Instead we had to wait outside another 90 minutes in 30 degree weather until our friends found us on their way out at the conclusion of the dance, clearly wondering what on earth had happened to us.

Was I breaking the Honor Code by wearing that dress? I didn't think so. I leave you to be the judge, but I can honestly say that I hate the BYU Honor Code. (Buckle up. Here comes a serious rant.)

Some time ago Brandon Davies was in the news, and at a time not too far-distant from now, some other BYU sports player will be in the news again. Why was Davies in the news? He had sex with his girlfriend. (Since when is a sports player having sex with their girlfriend news?)

There are so many things about the situation that upset me, including the following four points:

1. The world hailed BYU for having principles.
2. The news broadcast the fact that Davies was dismissed from BYU for having sex.
3. BYU insists on having a sports program.
4. The BYU Honor Code.

Notice I did not state anywhere on that list that Davies himself upset me. He didn't. He did exactly what every other guy his age does, except *he* was *selective*. I wasn't mad at Davies. He didn't spoil BYU's chances of winning championships; BYU spoiled their own chance of winning championships by trying to have a basketball team in the first place. But let's begin with point 1 before I launch into any tangents.

It irritates me that the sports world goes on and on about how amazing it is that BYU sticks to their principles. WOW, someone does what they say they'll do! *Is that really so unusual?* Mormons would love to argue *yes*, it *is* unusual; only Mormons live up to their word! But I know lots of people who aren't Mormon who live up to their word all the time, and lots of people who *are*, but *don't*. (I've been among them, sad to say.) Honestly, BYU *had* to be seen to boot Davies, whether they wanted to or not. He broke the Honor Code, so they *must* get rid of him. It's in the rule book, and if they're not living by their own rules, well, what sort of school is it? In fact, I might argue they dismissed him purely *because* of the press. Had they not dismissed him, the sports world would have been critical of BYU's cherry-picking, labeling them as so desperate to win games that they're willing to compromise their own morals. Since they did boot him, though, look at all the wonderful press it got them! Had the press never been made aware of Davies' sin, BYU might very well have overlooked the offense so that Davies could win them a championship.

In future, and to remedy point 1, Dear News Media: Please shut up.

While you're at it, News Media, please shut up about point 2 as well: if I want to know about the sex lives of basketball players, I'll read the police reports. I realize that the issue is that "all he did" was have sex with his girlfriend, and that most other college basketball players are not only seduced to specific universities with the promise of lots of sex, those universities *deliver!*, but I pity the man for what non-Mormons were thinking about him: "He signed on with a school that wouldn't let him have sex with his girlfriend? What a schmuck!" I also pity him for what Mormons were thinking about him *and* his girlfriend. It made me want to give that poor girl a hug. To have it broadcast to the sports world that you're sleeping with your boyfriend as a Mormon girl – and that that act denied BYU a championship win! – is tantamount to social suicide. Again, if the news media had just shut up, I wouldn't have had to hear about Brandon Davies' sex life.

Now to point 3: BYU, why on earth do you ever try to have sports teams? It is impossible to recruit people because of the Honor Code (unless they're Mormon), and isn't your motto "Enter to Learn, Go Forth to

Serve"? How are college sports programs in any way conducive to either education or service? If you're going to boot people for their sins, and let's face it, professional sports players are tempted far more regularly than the rest of us, why try to build a team in the first place?

I'll tell you why. BYU derives 3 major benefits from sports:

1. MONEY. Alumni don't love to donate; they love to attend games. They want their money behind a team they can root for, whether or not that team wins. BYU makes *bank* with their sports teams.

2. PUBLICITY. How better to get Mormons on national television in a positive light? Put their sports games on ESPN! We've had a couple hundred years of bad press, and learned with Romney's presidential run that we're still not very well liked or understood, but sports games are great for name recognition for the church.

3. If and when we *do* win, we give the Honor Code (and therefore *our religion*) credit. I'm not saying we go around chanting "God gave us a win!" Instead we say "Isn't it amazing that these terrific players managed this fabulous feat *without* the use of alcohol, cigarettes, coffee, tea, steroids, illegal drugs, crime, gambling, sex, or masturbation? That's what being Mormon is all about!"

I say: BYU, stop trying to have sports programs. (You won't, I know, but you have at least one BYU graduate who thinks less of you for trying to compete on a playing field with the rest of the world just for publicity, money, and bragging rights.)

Finally point 4, arguably the most controversial point: I HATE THE BYU HONOR CODE.

Years ago I left my home and family to embark on adulthood, to pursue higher education, and to make something of myself by myself. I went to BYU at the tender age of 18 and signed an Honor Code stating, in effect, that I would not sin. If I sinned, I risked losing my place at the university, not to mention any and all educational credits I had earned to that point. The Honor Code was my invisible parent, and all my friends and roommates became tattletale brothers and sisters. You can imagine how your average kid takes to the idea that Mommy and Daddy Religion are standing by ready to punish you. (I'm not talking about a Molly Mormon or Peter Priesthood kid; I'm talking about an 18 year-old who has never been away from home or out from under the wings of already over-protective parents.)

So BYU becomes a sort of Nazi Germany-style Fascist State, with the Honor Code Office the Gestapo and your roommates (and sometimes friends) the Hitler Youth, ready to rat you out for any infraction.

But the real problem is that *the Honor Code is not in line with the gospel of Jesus Christ.*

The scriptures say we are all sinners. Each of us inherently carries within us the "natural man" and, therefore, a proclivity for carnal things. Sort of an instinct to sin, if you will. We also have our conscience, which Mormons would argue is the Spirit of Christ we carry with us to direct us in proper paths.

But we are sinful creatures. Each of us. No matter how righteous we try to be, the scriptures say we are miserable sinners with no business being saved. Yet, what happens? Christ saves us! He says to come unto Him, love Him, try to be like Him, give ourselves to Him, and no matter how big a sinner, failure, or schmuck we may be (I'm paraphrasing here; I don't remember Jesus ever calling anyone a schmuck), He and He alone has redeemed us, bought and paid for our souls.

When we screw up – because we *will* – we turn to Him to repent.

The Honor Code office tells us to repent, fine, but we also need to come talk to *them* about our sins so they can determine whether or not to kick us out of college.

Wait, what?

I thought repentance was between me and God, not between me and someone the Honor Code Office has assigned to my "case." You see, the Honor Code Office is judge, jury, and executioner. Once you've been reported, you're called in – without being given *any* information as to *why* you *must* appear, who turned you in, or what they said – and finally the charges made against you are disclosed. You have a chance to have your say, and while they are not inflexible, the Honor Code Office is definitely (and intentionally) intimidating. Try, by the way, going back to your apartment later that night to sleep in the same place at the roommates who turned you in. (*Yes*, I speak from experience.)

Also, if you know what the consequences will be of anyone finding out you screwed up in some area of your life, how many people imagine those consequences are encouragement to make themselves right with God? Did, after Brandon Davies had sex with his girlfriend, he think to himself "Ooh, I'm so excited to go to my bishop and confess and repent and be called in to the Honor Code Office and thrown out of school and publicly lambasted!'"? I think not.

My guess is he was turned in. Only an idiot or a martyr (crushed by their own twisted guilt) would take the aforementioned course of action. What if he was truly repentant? What if he really just couldn't stand the guilt and wanted to repent, no matter the repercussions? While that may be true, he's still an idiot (in my opinion). No one in their right mind would *not* delay repentance for a shot at MVP in a winning championship game. He was in it to make the NBA, so let's be realistic: When you *know* the consequences (and because of the Honor Code, the consequences are *dire*), you naturally delay repentance. Unless you're reported, in which case you're screwed. But BYU has set you up (via the Honor Code) to *be* reported. (That's actually part of the Honor Code. You have a "responsibility" to "help" your fellow students adhere to the Honor Code and keep "worthy" of their place at BYU by reporting them to the Honor Code should they flub up. *Seriously.*)

I remember reading a comment on an online news story about Brandon Davies that said, "If you can't follow the Honor Code, you shouldn't be at BYU."

Really? I don't remember Jesus Christ walking around Galilee telling people that if they were sinners, they shouldn't convert to Christianity. In fact, it seems to me that most of the people He hung out with were sinners. But BYU has a higher standard, right? *Higher than Christ Himself?* Can you imagine Christ saying "Be like Me, but if you can't hang, you should just settle for hell and damnation right now!"? I don't mean to be glib or blasphemous, but we act as though someone must be perfect to be counted among potential BYU grads. We must sign and live by the Honor Code and remain without sin – one of which sins is wearing shorts an inch above the knee – in order to be worthy of that degree.

We are *not* perfect. We are *sinners*. *That* is why we're supposed to *need* Christ. But the Honor Code sort of negates all that. Our hope of being saved may still be through Christ, but our hope of being saved *and educated at His University* is by following the Honor Code.

I have to jump back to modesty for a moment: Once upon a time I unintentionally caused quite a stir at BYU. I had been perusing the job boards looking for something that wasn't janitorial work, and I noticed an ad in the Universe – the name of the BYU newspaper, ironically – seeking art class models. I applied, *was issued a bikini*, and started modeling for on-campus classes for $6.50 per hour. It was a profoundly easy job for me. I could sit and think for 20 minutes, take a five minute break, sit and think for another 20 minutes, and so on for each three hour class. I became a favorite of a few of the professors and began modeling regularly – and then exclusively – for their masters' classes.

At about the same time an art supply store in Provo opened a loft studio above the store, and one of the BYU professors for whom I modeled ask if I'd be interested in modeling for the very same students for substantially more pay once a week…in the nude.

Modesty has never been my forte. The offer intrigued me, and since BYU was already paying me to break the Honor Code (and issued me the bikini to do it!), I figured it wasn't much different. Besides, I knew the professor (and his wife and a son) quite well, and I also knew what a difficult time his students were having when they attended nude sessions at the Springville Art Museum. Students who did *fabulous* work in class were bringing back crap from Springville, and the professor figured out it was because the bikini was a sort of "wrapping guide" as artists tried to shade around body curves. A nude offered no such artistic support. Additionally, without nudes in their portfolio, virtually none of the students would ever get a real-world job, so they were forced to go elsewhere.

Having modeled many times for him, I knew the professor would never expect me to pose in any way that could be misconstrued as even remotely sexual, and he never did. I modeled quite a few times for that class, earned all the money I needed for my books for two full semesters, and even had a good laugh with a dozen or so students over the scene from Titanic where Kate Winslet's character says that being drawn by Leonardo DeCaprio's character was one of the most erotic moments of her life. "Yeah," I told them, "right now my butt's asleep, I can't feel my left leg, I have a kink in my neck and I'd kill to stretch my back, plus I'm sitting here wondering just how visible my unshaven leg hair is to all of you married BYU students. Definitely the most erotic moment of *my* life!"

One day a roommate caught wind of my off-campus modeling, got together with my other roommates to compile a list of grievances, and reported me to the Honor Code. At the same time she wrote an editorial about me to the BYU Universe, and though she did not mention my name, she signed her editorial with her own name, making it painfully obvious to everyone in our apartment complex (and therefore everyone in our ward) exactly to whom she referred. A professor and a few students wrote editorials to the Universe in my defense, and the professor with whom I worked wrote a dissertation to university leadership, explaining the situation and his take on the necessity of drawing from the nude.

He and four other masters' students were dismissed from the university. In combination with my "other sins", and two months before graduation, I was expelled. Eight months later I was readmitted to BYU, but only after weekly meetings with my bishop to prove I was "on the right track" and a tearful final apology at both my "court of love" hearing and my Honor Code hearing.

Did I ever, even for one moment, regret modeling for art classes? Not once. Did I ever regret the actions taken by my self-righteous roommates? Immensely, though there was nothing I could do except "repent".

Incidentally, that same professor had done a painting of me from the nude that was absolutely glorious. A few years ago my husband tracked down the professor and offered to buy the painting, but the professor, kind and generous as always, just popped it in the mail. My husband, at first wary of the idea that I had ever posed nude, was so enchanted by the beautiful painting that he had it professionally framed, and it now hangs in our bedroom, my young, pre-baby body immortalized on canvas.

Thank you, dear Brother Professor. You were a dream to work for. All my best to you, your sweet wife, and your amazing family.

While at BYU, I felt a distance betwixt myself and my peers, professors, and leaders…you can imagine. I called and chatted with a friend from back home about it one night, and must've been especially depressed-sounding, talking about how I wish I could just be done at BYU. He severely misinterpreted my statements, calling back a little while later to check on me. Turns out that after talking with him, I decided to take a walk…at night…to the campus library. (This was not unusual for me. The library was open late, and sitting amongst the shelves always had a stabilizing influence.)

When he called, I was gone. He alerted my roommates to my depression and asked them to track me down, so they travelled from apartment to apartment to see where I had gone, but had no luck finding me. My friend then called my parents, who could also not get a hold of me. He then decided to call the police to track me down.

No, really.

When I returned to my apartment an hour or two later, my roommates were all in tears, and one raced out to the parking lot to inform the officer sitting out there in his car that I was safely home. He brought me down to his car and had a long and patronizing chat with me about how I shouldn't worry my friends, family, and roommates that way, and that if I was indeed depressed, I needed professional help. I noted that *I* had *not* worried my family or roommates – my friend had taken that responsibility upon himself – but that I would consider seeing a counselor. I was told I had no choice; in order for the officer to release me back to my life, I would have to agree to see a counselor and report back to the police with the counselor's name and contact information.

The next day I headed to the student center to seek counseling, set up my first session for later that afternoon, then called the station to report to the officer the name and contact information for my counselor. He thanked me and told me my case was dismissed. I was tempted not to bother with the counselor, but as I've never been one to disobey authority (thanks to my Mormon upbringing), and I wouldn't want trouble if the officer contacted the counselor later, I attended my session that afternoon.

My counselor seemed like a nice-enough guy. I told him I struggled a bit where the church was concerned, and that's what I had been trying to express to my friend: BYU just didn't seem like a good fit for me. He was very understanding, and as I left, he set up a follow-up appointment for two days later. I showed again, hoping the session would close my proverbial book. Halfway through the session I explained that one of my difficulties was my sex drive. It was rough for me to attend a school that, like church, made me feel evil for wanting to have sex.

It was then that the conversation changed, almost imperceptibly at first. A few minutes later he told me about a former patient of his who stood up in the middle of one of their sessions and took off her top, then sat on his lap and informed him that she had wanted to sleep with him since their first session. I was amazed, but not by how inappropriate *his* comments were. I only thought (in complete shock), "Wow, she did that?!"

From that point forward I tried to discern the reason he might have told me about the incident, never imagining that it might not have actually happened. At the end of the session he squeezed my arm and pulled me to him, gave me a hug, and ran his hand down my back in an intimate fashion, asking me when I was available for our next session. I told him I thought he had already helped me tremendously and assured him I was cured. The disappointment on his face was clear, but I still thank my lucky stars that he did not push, and that I never had to return to his office.

Before you ask, no, I never reported him. After all (to my beleaguered mind), he didn't press the issue of my returning for additional sessions, and perhaps I'd misunderstood his story and misinterpreted his actions…right? Anyway, who would believe an LDS psychologist at the Y had ever done anything questionable? Plus, he had a wife and family to support; could I really accuse him of being inappropriate and endanger both his livelihood and family if I wasn't 100% sure he'd done anything wrong? (Sigh.)

Because my time under BYU's thumb represents such a huge chunk of my adult life and my personal development, I must relate one additional "leadership" experience before moving on. My freshman year in college – at the conclusion of which I wrote that five-page letter to my bishop – was profoundly difficult for a number of reasons, but most of all because of my bishop. He already did not like me when I stepped into his office two weeks before the end of the semester, and here's why:

A couple months into school I knew almost all the girls on my dorm floor. Three of them were a little on the pudgy side, and they were all beautiful, talented, brilliant women. Each came to me in turn during the course of one single week, two of them in tears, and one mad as hell. Each reported separately that, during an interview with our bishop, he had advocated anorexia, bulimia, or a combination of the two, explaining they were going to have to "skinny up" if ever they wanted to "catch a husband."

I was outraged, having had a number of friends suffer either anorexia or bulimia (or both) during high school. I could not fathom that a priesthood leader had advocated for something so profoundly stupid and unhealthy, and I made an appointment to meet with him. When he asked why I made the interview we were sitting through, I explained that some of the girls on my floor had told me he encouraged them to engage in anorexia and/or bulimia in order to win husbands. I also explained *I believed they had misinterpreted his admonitions*, but felt the need to warn him that some of his female membership believed he wanted them to starve themselves or binge and purge. I then sat back, waiting for a look that would indicate his horror at their misinterpretation.

Instead *he* sat forward in his chair, fingertips together on the desk in front of him. "Young lady," he began, "who do you think you are to question the revelation I receive from the Lord on behalf of the individuals in my ward?"

I must've been just as ashen-faced as I was utterly speechless.

"I never," he continued, "*never* expect to see you in my office again, unless it's with an apology for having questioned my authority." He glared at me for just a moment, and then said, "You may go."

After considerable tears and prayer, I decided maybe I wasn't in the wrong, and perhaps I should try again. I set up an appointment with the stake president – the man just above our bishop in the line of priesthood authority – a couple days later. After explaining the situation (and my bishop's response) to him, he sat back, nodding. Finally he spoke.

"You know, sister, I genuinely think your intentions were good, coming to me about this, but they're also a bit misguided. I feel very strongly that the Lord wants me to call you to repentance. Your bishop has been chosen by God and granted His power and authority here on earth – the priesthood – to oversee the members of his ward, yourself included. Not only have you challenged him, you've now gone over his head to challenge him *again*. Your bishop was right. I think you need to repent, and it's my duty to call you to repentance here and now. Your bishop knows best for his ward members. No matter how much you think you know, I assure you, you have *no* authority where your friends are concerned. I think it's best you leave that to your bishop."

Shocking as all that was, what more could I have expected when "apostle" Dallin H. Oaks tells us that "It's wrong to criticize leaders of the church, even if the criticism is true"?

Even if the criticism is true. Apparently their direct pipeline to God via the priesthood not only makes up for any idiocy on their part, it actually *negates* it.

I dropped the matter. After all, that's what I was taught to do by my faith. *Drop it.* Apply cognitive dissonance. *Move on.*

But I couldn't move *away* from BYU. I still needed to find a husband, after all! It was the summer after my sophomore year at BYU (I often went year-round) that I was first proposed to. I was living in an apartment off campus, and a new crop of students moved in and out of our complex after each semester. We had an unusually large influx of boys that summer, and I was thrilled. One of them was named...Tom? Tim? Trent? Now I remember...but let's go with Trent. (The guy proposed to me, and I had to *seriously* think about what his name was just now!) Trent and I ended up in the same Family Home Evening group, known as "FHE." While Family Home Evening in a real family usually consists of an actual family, at BYU groups are decided by the wards, and a Mom and Dad of the group are designated. My FHE Dad introduced me to Trent, and he was incredibly good-looking, apparently thinking I was, too.

We spent time together on and off for two weeks, but I just wasn't connecting with him. One night he took me on an elaborate date: a friend of his had a pilot's license and a Cessna, and the three of us went on a flight over Utah Lake, (there were flowers on the back seat of the plane, where I sat,) circling over and over and doing touch-and-go's. Had we actually been *going* somewhere, I might have enjoyed it more, but after the sixth touch-and-go, I was a tad bit bored. They were chatting in front, but my stomach was thrown by the constant up-and-down, and when we finally got back to my apartment, I had less-than-zero interest in the pizza he ordered for us. He put on one of his favorite movies, the truly terrible Avengers with Uma Thurman and Sean Connery, while I lay writhing on the couch, trying to control my stomach. Halfway through the movie he hit pause, got down on one knee, and proposed. I told him I wasn't ready for that sort of commitment after only two weeks. He nodded, pressed play on the movie, and when it finished, snatched up his movie and leftover pizza and went home. We did not go out again, but when I next saw him, he had a new girl on his arm, so I'm fairly certain neither of us considered it a great loss.

I turned down one other "proposal" that I also did not consider a great loss. Like my friend Beth, whose boss offered her a "position" as second wife, I, too, have met with a second-wife proposal. The circumstances were particularly odd, so please bear with me; this will probably seem as strange to you as it did to me.

My friends, who we will call Peter and Sara, met and wooed during the course of two years while they lived in my apartment complex. I was friends with them both, and it happened that Sara shared my major. Peter graduated from BYU about four months before the following incident, and was gainfully employed in Spanish Fork, 20 minutes south of Provo. They bought a house in Spanish Fork, and one day I ran into Sara on campus and she invited me over to see their home and have dinner with them. I was thrilled for them, and since I hadn't seen them since their wedding, I promised to make myself available the very next afternoon.

They lived in a home owners' association with a common pool, so she and I went swimming shortly after she picked me up. Once back in their home, and considering my ambivalence toward modesty, I thought nothing of showering in the all-glass shower in her master bath while she hopped in the tub. The layout of the master bath was like a long hallway, the shower nearest the bedroom door, and the tub at the other end of the room. We chatted, everything was just fine, and then...Peter walked in. "Hey, 'Gina!" he said, smiling as though I were fully dressed and seated on the couch instead of totally exposed and washing my hair. He passed right by me and came to rest on the bathtub edge, where he made out with his wife, then sat on the tub's rim, shooting the breeze with two naked women, one his wife, and the other in complete shock.

I rinsed as quickly as possible – honestly, I can't tell you why I didn't run screaming from the room – and asked for a towel, my un-embarrass-able cheeks bright, screaming red. Peter grabbed one off the counter, walked over to me so we were face to face with only the glass door between us, and reached over the door to hand me the towel.

Sara got out of the tub then, and disappeared with her husband into the bedroom to change, so I closed the door and took my sweet time getting dressed...or, rather, took my sweet time sitting on the toilet lid trying to figure out my next move after I'd dressed at the speed of light.

I cannot say for certain, but I'm pretty sure Peter and Sara had sex while I was busy staying safely locked in the bathroom. The room reeked of it, and Sara was *still* dressing when I emerged from the protection of the master bath. They insisted I stay for dinner, and though I protested that I had a TON of homework and had to get back to work on it, they had the car keys, so they won.

The conversation was strained on my end, but they both appeared quite normal as they prepared our meal in their kitchen. Once we sat down to dinner, Peter offered the blessing on the meal, then announced they had recently joined a fundamentalist branch of the church...and that they were hoping to make me part of their family.

    *By the way, and because I have GOT to talk about something else for just a minute, and you probably require an explanation, today we have the LDS church (the Mormons), the RLDS church (the Reorganized church, now call the Church of Christ, which splintered off when the saints left for Utah and those believers who did NOT want to participate in polygamy stayed behind), and the FLDS church (the Fundamentalist church, which splintered off when the saints announced that polygamy would no longer be practiced, but they *continued* practicing the "principle"). The Church of Christ is based back East, while the FLDS church is the one you likely hear about on the new, in Texas, Arizona, Utah, and the like.*

    What was my reply? I hardly remember exactly what I said, but I know I thanked them for the offer, and for considering me someone they'd want to, um, be married to, and assured them that I was still a practicing *traditional* Mormon, but if ever that changed and I joined the FLDS church, I'd let them know.

    I don't remember eating dinner, I don't remember what they said, I don't even remember the ride home, or who drove me. (I think it must've been Sara, but I honestly couldn't tell you.) I only remember a roommate asking me how my dinner-date went, and me opening my mouth to speak, then closing it again and disappearing into my room for what was probably my ONLY 8 PM bedtime during the whole of my college experience.

Post-BYU

    My post-BYU experience starts with my marriage, which is wonderful. It hasn't always been, and like all couples we've hit some major rough patches – not the least of which is my leaving the church – but we're okay, and I adore my husband. I also complain about him every once in a while to only one other person in the entire world; she, as my best friend, does the same, and she can attest to the fact that my husband and I don't always have the perfect relationship. I can equally attest to that same fact where she and her husband are concerned. We seldom bitch about our spouses, honestly, but sometimes something comes up where one of us just needs to vent, and the other listens without judgment because we know our relationship with our own husband, while wonderful, is not always ideal. (Disclaimer, disclaimer; on with the tale!)

That said, one instance in her marital relationship is indicative of the typical Utah Mormon marriage, so I hope that, if and when she someday reads this, she takes no offense to my using her as an example. (I'm sure she could use me as an example of a great many dysfunctional behaviors, should she choose to.)

Let's call her Alicia, and her husband Aaron. Aaron runs the family finances, even though Alicia's education and fiscal competency outshines Aaron in the financial area of their relationship. He has made a number of decisions for their family, including what to buy, where to move, which job to take and under what circumstances, that she did not agree with, and which choices she would not have made on her own. In the same breath she explains that, just as the gospel says, her priesthood-holder husband is entitled to revelation for their family in all areas including financial decisions, and while he considers her input, the final decision is his. Many times she has remarked that "she just has to trust that her husband is following the Spirit", and the consequences of his decisions will be his to deal with. That's all well and good, of course, but Aaron has made a few profoundly foolish business decisions. While his pride may suffer, it is *Alicia and family* who are forced to deal with the consequences.

At one point he explained that his boss's old business partner had a home he had abandoned to foreclosure, and that if they were to move in – rent-free – they could stay there indefinitely since they would have a "rental contract" from his boss. Alicia and her friends spent nearly a hundred man-hours cleaning the thoroughly-trashed home to make it livable, moved all their earthly belongings into it (Alicia was pregnant at the time), and settled in, her parents painting and decorating a nursery for their new grandbaby.

A month after the baby was born the home foreclosed, and they had exactly three days to be out, with no place to go. (They had rented their condo to another family, using the rent to make their mortgage payment; meanwhile, Aaron's boss had not been paying him "because he couldn't afford to," and their living rent-free was supposed to make up for his boss's inability to pay for Aaron's services.)

Another friend we'll call Trish is an author. This has proved a bone of contention for her husband in one specific area: in order to keep up with the literary world, she has been required to wade through books he'd prefer she did not read, specifically 50 Shades of Gray, part of the erotica genre.

The decision to keep on top of the bestseller reading list did not bode well for Trish, who discovered, much to her great and reasonable dismay, that her spouse had been so distressed by her decision to read the 50 Shades series, he had gone to their bishop for counsel about what to do with his wife's smut-dabbling.

(He, by the way, had spent time battling his own soft porn addiction, and was therefore unequipped to handle her reading anything from the erotica genre.) The bishop, thank heavens, told him it was really nothing to worry about, and that her need to stay on top of new releases was clearly important to her career. (If anything, I'm fairly certain he actually *benefitted* from her reading!) He headed home, confessing to his wife that he had confessed *her* sin to the bishop in order to seek counsel and clarification, unsure as to his own priesthood responsibility in this situation.

After coming to terms with the anger, hurt, and resentment Trish felt in response to her husband's disclosing her "sin", she finally simmered down, informed me that she knew he was just "doing his best to lead their family and protect them from temptation," and all was well once more.

It doesn't always work out so well for others. Two couples from my childhood ward have struggled dramatically, as has the aforementioned "Virgin Lips Lady". One of the couples hired me to babysit regularly, and I knew them well. He cheated on her with one of the women he home-taught, and when she discovered she'd been wronged, proceeded to beat him as best she could, being half his size. He had her arrested, pressed charges for battery, and – here it comes – ultimately *she took him back.*

The second couple had been married 10 years – *with four kids* – when he slept with his secretary, and it took him years to make it back into full fellowship with the church, but she forgave him. In fact, they had *two more children.* 20 years after he was reinstated he cheated again, over 30 years into their marriage. Most people believe they have divorced, but the reality is that they are permanently separated, an arrangement that permits them to remain "sealed" as a family so that her children and grandchildren will "retain those blessings." I often wonder exactly how tortuous that is for her.

The virgin lips lady's story is equally awful. She did not hear of her husband's infidelity during their engagement until her eldest was 11 years old, when the other woman unceremoniously dumped her 12 year-old daughter on their doorstep, stating that she could no longer care for the girl. In a matter of a few short moments, everyone's world came crashing down: the 12 year-old, who had never known her father, was now expected to live in his home with his wife and family, chasing desperately after her mother as she drove away and left her daughter there alone. She had been raised *very* differently than the other children in this ultra-LDS family, and for a million reasons did not mesh with them.

The mother, a drug-addict, disappeared for the next six months. The husband's affair was revealed in the worst possible way, and was forced by his wife to take a paternity test, confirming that the 12 year-old was indeed his daughter. The eldest child of the family, a boy, (they are Polynesian; the eldest, particularly when male, is amazingly revered in their culture,) had been displaced as eldest by a female stranger. Virgin Lips Lady caught as much of the brunt of the whole thing as the newly-discovered daughter. Suddenly everything she knew about her husband seemed a lie, her son was no longer her husband's eldest, and they were forced to accept a sixth child into their home, being that the girl had no place else to go. All this, and we have not even touched on what this means in the LDS church.

The husband had to undergo church disciplinary action, but he was eventually reinstated to full fellowship. His wife took in the girl, did her best (but failed miserably) trying not to resent the child, and though absolutely devastated by the situation, forgave and stood by her husband. They had the girl with them on and off until she was 18, when she decided to start her own life, and their eldest son now attends BYU.

One would hope all those marriages had been based on something positive to begin with, but that's not always the case: Likely because they are young, innocent, unsullied fresh meat, freshman girls get a lot of attention at BYU. Fully half a dozen girls of the 88 in my freshman ward were married by the end of freshman year at 18 years of age. After I graduated from BYU I worked in an office building. One of my co-workers was a 27 year-old man who was *very* eager to marry (having just attained "menace to society" status), and announced to the entire office that he was seeking a "cute" 18 year-old, asking us to set him up with any we might know. I asked him to define cute, and his answer amazed me: "You know, hot. Cute. As a button. Big puppy dog eyes, one of those cute giggly girls that says funny things and basically needs an older man to worship." (*I kid you not.*)

I was appalled, but managed to ask about her intellectual requirements when curiosity finally got the best of me. "Not too smart," came his reply. "I don't need someone smarter than me. I need someone who will make me laugh [ostensibly *at* her], take care of my house, skip out on her garments when I want her in panties, and give me cute kids." That, ladies and gentlemen, was his standard. A year later, at 28, he married an 18 year-old adorable, bouncy blonde girl from Georgia, a freshman at BYU. I have no idea what became of them.

Speaking of garments, I don't wear mine anymore. I don't believe they are necessary, that they protect me from anything (except my husband's sex drive), nor do I want to be reminded of the peculiar and alarming temple ceremonies garments are supposed to make members recall. I am occasionally forced to fake wearing them (read: to church), but I always feel stupid when I do, not to mention it severely limits my wear-to-church wardrobe. I have some truly fabulous clothes that would be stunning in a dressed-up setting, but since my shoulders show or the bottom two inches of my thighs are visible, I'm relegated to the same three boring outfits. At least I can wear a thong under them, and no one is the wiser.

Some time ago I was getting dressed for church, slipping on my G's (the BYU nickname for garments), and my husband stood back to check me out. Now, I realize that "garments" and "check out" don't really seem to go together…no, they don't. I can't justify it, they just don't. Anyway, he's standing back, checking me out, and no sooner does he point out my Camel Toe (thanks to the fact that the waistband of my G's sits about an inch from my bosom – one "small" fits all "smalls"!) than he ventures forth with the following: "Know that would make those things even sexier?"

I came up with one of my wittiest replies to date: "If they were one-piece?"

"No, well, I guess that might help. But there's one thing that would make them so sexy, I'd be ready to go, right now."

"And that is?"

"Grab a bra – any bra, but preferably a colorful one – and put that baby on *over* your garments. *That* would be the ULTIMATE."

So, like always, I did. He winked at me, and I wasn't sure whether to laugh, cry, or vomit, but that was the beginning of the end of garments for me, because yes, we *are* supposed to wear our bras *over* our garments. I know there are women who claim that it's a personal decision, but the reality is that the church's stance on women's garment tops is that they are to be worn *under* brassieres. *Really.*

I've never been a fan of garments, not because they're ugly, but because of how crazy they make us look to outsiders. My dear friend who we'll call Jainy, who I met while we were coworkers in Utah, is not a member of the church. We were chatting one day about my being a member – she told me that she struggled to believe I was Mormon, since I had been willing to become friends with her, (what a *sad* commentary on Utahns!) – and she made a crack about garments, explaining that she and her friends called them "Jesus Jammies." I laughed myself sick, but deep down I thought, *Ugh. What am I doing wearing these stupid things? Even a non-member knows that sacred underpants are ridiculous!*

That said, my very first – and very worst – blow as a garment-wearer came *on my wedding day*. My friend (I'll call her) Dixie and I had grown up together, friends and neighbors since we were 12. On the day I was married, my husband and I arrived at our own reception about 20 minutes late, thanks to major traffic on the way back from the temple. I had to change back into my wedding dress, and Dixie volunteered to help me zip up, so we disappeared into the church bathroom together (the reception took place at an LDS chapel) and I stripped down to my garments and bra, thinking nothing of it.

Dixie looked like I had hit her over the head with a baseball bat.

I quickly laughed off my garments, explaining that I was now an endowed member of the church, and she helped zip up my dress, chuckling nervously. She left the reception 10 minutes later.

We saw each other once after I had my first child, but things weren't the same, and though I've tried a few times over the years to get back in touch with her, left messages, sent emails and the like, I never hear back. I don't take it personally – we were great friends growing up, and I know we could be still – but I do indeed resent my childhood religion for it. I know the sight of me in my garments terrified her, and I don't blame her: her friend had joined a cult.

Dearest Dixie, I honestly didn't realize at the time that God doesn't require me to wear sacred underwear in order for Him to take me back. Please chalk it up to how I was raised. I'd love to be able to strike up a friendship again. Bottom line: I'd been duped.

I'd also duped others, like the teenage girl who, when I was student-teaching, came in the Monday after it was announced in General Conference that women were only supposed to wear one set of pierced earrings, having removed all but one of her earrings. She had had 7 piercings in one ear, and 6 in the other, but when she heard the edict, she immediately went into her bathroom and removed all but one earring in each ear, letting her holes close up.

Now, I'm not a huge fan of multiple piercings, (or tattoos, for that matter,) but that's *entirely personal*. If others want to pierce (and tat and decorate) themselves all over and in quantity, that's their prerogative. But this young woman impressed me. Why? Not because she had thought about the situation for herself and studied the edict out in her mind, not because she had stuck to her guns and done what made her most happy, but because she had heard the "will of the Lord", who apparently felt that the number of earrings the women of His church chose to wear was important enough to have a Prophet convey His limit, and obeyed without question.

THAT impressed me. I lauded her, in fact, for blindly following the prophet's instructions. I used her as an honored example with my own young women when I was YW's president.

And *again*, I am ashamed. Earrings are inappropriate, but blind obedience is awesome?! Let's cover some MORE "inappropriates": A friend from my Utah days has a younger sister, now in Young Women's. Her sister returned home a couple months ago with the project she and her peers had been assigned to work on for their YW activity that night: each cut out an immodestly-dressed fashion model from a magazine, glued the model onto construction paper, and then combed through the available magazines for "appropriate" clothing, finally putting together a modest outfit and gluing it on to the model to cover up her immodesty. (If you're a Mormon reading this book – not that any would – I fear I may have sparked a new idea for an upcoming YW's activity. *Eek*!) There are so *infinitely* many things wrong with this, I'm not sure where to begin, so perhaps I'll leave off on the discussion by stating only the *most* obvious: Since when did we begin expecting others to live up to our standards? Since when did we stop accepting people for who they are – whoever that is – and decide it was our job to change them…all the way down to their very clothing? Since when did we start teaching teens that they are "better"

160

than their infinitely more-experienced and ultra-successful fashion-industry-mogul elders, just because they understand (what we've told them is) "truth"?

Oh, wait. Since *always*.

I have a friend in our current ward whose daughter approached her in tears after church. When she asked what was wrong, her daughter explained they had had a lesson on modesty, and she now knew it was *wrong* to wear dresses without sleeves. It just so happened she was wearing her old Easter dress that Sunday, and though the straps were easily three inches wide, it had *no sleeves*. She then explained that she had been humiliated by her own appearance, angry with her parents for permitting her to wearing immodest clothing in public, *let alone to church!*, and she would never wear *anything* without sleeves *ever again*.

Her daughter is 8.

I had a similar experience myself. My elder child pulled me aside one evening before bed, having just read "The Friend," an LDS kids' magazine. "Mom," began the conversation, "the Friend says women should be modest." (At the time I was wearing a sundress with spaghetti straps. It was August, and I had given up my garments some time before.)

"Okay," I said simply, waiting.

"It says women can't show their shoulders because it's wrong."

I smiled. "Okay." Silence. Finally I continued. "So you want to know, if the Friend says I shouldn't show my shoulders, why I'm showing my shoulders?" I was met with a head nod. "Honey," I explained, "I'm a grown up, and I make decisions for myself based on what *I* believe to be right. Its summertime, I'm hot, our house is hot, and I feel most comfortable in a dress like this."

"But the prophet says – "

"I know what the prophet says, and I know what the Friend says, but you will learn as you grow up that Mommy doesn't always agree with everything the Friend says. Mommy also doesn't always agree with everything the prophet says." I looked down at my sweet child and squeezed an arm. "Tell me something."

"Okay?"

"Do you think Heavenly Father still loves me, even with my shoulders showing?"

"Yes."

"Do you think Heavenly Father still loves me, even if I disagree with the prophet?"

"Yes."

"Then I think you and I have nothing to worry about."

That settled the issue. I confess, I almost feel like I got lucky, particularly considering the heartbreaking fact that I'm currently still raising a couple of Mormons.

It wasn't any easier with the Mormon kids I taught, back when I was more career-minded.

Having taught in a Utah school, I can honestly say that if I *never* teach again, it will be too soon. My difficulty was not so much the students, though they contributed: I had a 12 year-old student who had been raped on the football field by a 13 year-old boy, a girl whose father (an LDS bishop) had been molesting her since she was 8, an atheist 14 year-old boy with one friend in the entire world, and a pair of 12 year-old girls who introduced me to the horrifying world of "cutting"; each had a series of self-inflicted slices on their arms that they hid with long sleeves, even in the dead of summer, and they explained that it was the only way they had found to cleanse themselves of their guilt for various sins they had committed that weren't severe-enough to confess to a bishop.

This is only a sampling, mind you. I saw and heard more in my years as a teacher than I can ever hope to express, let alone process.

My difficulty, instead, was my students' parents. The first week of school I introduced my class to a bit of Shakespeare, considering we would be covering Romeo and Juliet, and the very next week one of my students disappeared from class. When I asked after her, an administrator informed me that her parents had called the school about me, complaining that I was addressing topics – specifically suicide – in class, and that they could not bear for their sweet 14 year-old girl to think about such wicked things, so they had demanded she be pulled from my class.

A couple months later I was in the middle of a lesson when a parent walked into my classroom, seeking a conversation. She would not be dissuaded, even considering (at that very moment!) I was in the middle of teaching. I assigned a short reading and advised the class that I needed five minutes, during which time they could break into groups to discuss the theme of a reading. I then went directly outside the door to chat with the woman. She informed me her daughter had explained that another student had read aloud a short story he had written that included a murderous demon character. I remembered the story well; the student had received an A for his amazing creativity.

The woman told me how deeply offended she was that I would allow a young teenager to write – and then share! – a tale containing such dark and obscene overtones, and that I might as well have been advocating NECROMANCY. Yes, she used the word necromancy. She demanded to know what grade I gave the student, and whether or not I had corrected him for presenting such sick and disturbing work. I replied that he had received top marks, that I knew him to be a brilliant and creative youth, and I was proud of his skill. I then escorted her to the front office, informing the secretaries that this mother had interrupted my class with a complaint better-heard by an administrator, and left her to it.

My favorite incident, however, occurred during my first-ever parent-teacher conference. The mother of one of my students sat down to chat, but looked incredibly agitated, so I asked what might be the matter. She ranted for a minute about a teenager she'd seen in the hall, explaining that the girl couldn't have been older than 14, but that she was *wearing makeup*, and that when the young lady bent over to pick something up from the floor, the woman had seen the girl's stomach *peeking out*!

I said something like "Wow, really?" and then asked the woman which of my students was her child. When she mentioned her daughter by name, I almost hit the floor. Two days earlier her daughter had come to me (it was a Monday morning) and revealed that she feared, at 12, that she might be pregnant. Her period had only begun a few months before, but that weekend she had gotten incredibly drunk and had sex.

At 12.

It gets worse: not only did she fear she was pregnant from her weekend of drunken sex, she then revealed that she wasn't sure *how many boys* she had sex with…or even *who they were*.

I had directed her to the school counselor, not knowing how to handle the situation myself, yet here sat her mother in the chair opposite mine complaining of a 14 year-old girl wearing lipstick and exposing an inch of belly when she moved just-so.

Incidentally, I was not allowed to say anything to the mother about her daughter's actions the prior weekend, as per the school counselor (whose job it was to handle the situation). I learned years later that the girl had eventually come out of the closet as a feminist lesbian, and had her name removed from the church rolls at the same time.

Just because I think it's time for a laugh: I had a student in Utah who was an atheist. (In all my time teaching, I had a total of four self-professed atheists and/or agnostics. *One* felt socially accepted.) I'll call him David. He was a kick. Upon our collective return from the Thanksgiving holiday – and with December looming – David walked into my classroom one day when it was just me and proclaimed, "I fucking hate Christmas!"

I confess, I hadn't expected this. It wasn't that I hadn't heard such language before, it was just that David had always seemed so even-tempered and sweet. Normally he was, but that day something had set him off.

"Okay, kiddo, what's wrong?" I asked, bracing myself.

"It's just such bullshit!" he yelled, then took a deep breath and flopped into a chair. "It's like this every year. Everyone gets all fake-happy and syrupy-sweet. They smile more, they say hello, they hold doors, but then we get to the New Year and suddenly nobody gives a shit. They opened up their gifts, ate their big meals, decorated their trees, and when everything's cleaned up and put away, people like me suddenly drop off the face of the earth again. It's all FAKE!"

I then made a point that he couldn't get around: "Hey, you're an atheist, right? Do you still get presents for Christmas?"

"Well, yeah."

"Then I say you get to enjoy a month where people are finally nice, you get a bunch of brand new stuff, and when it's all said and done, you're still you...and you're *not* Mormon."

He had a good laugh, let out a sigh, and headed off to class.

But I heard you, David...loud and clear.

I only wish I'd heard one of my sisters loud and clear back when she left the church (after two semesters at what was then Ricks College, and is now BYU-Idaho). After sitting through a religion class where the professor discussed God's having once been a man like us (having progressed to be the God He now is), she began to imagine a very righteous Mormon character she called "Truck Driver Bob" who worked his way up through the priesthood on his own God's planet until he finally died and went to the Celestial Kingdom, continuing to progress until he himself became God and created worlds of (now "His") His own.

She approached her professor and asked him if it was indeed possible that God was once Truck Driver Bob, confused that the Alpha and Omega, with no beginning and no end, could actually have once been a truck driver. She also noted that that meant there might have been more than one Truck Driver Bob – maybe Truck Drivers Tom and Jerry, too – and that they, as well, became God of their own planets, meaning that there was more than one God…which would make us polytheistic.

Her professor explained that yes, God might once have been Truck Driver Bob, (or "Truck Driver Elohim," he corrected her!) but that after billions of years, He had progressed to become God, and since he began as an intelligence floating in space (more or less) and was "born" into a "spirit body" via his Heavenly Father and Mother, and continued on now as God, He had neither beginning nor end.

Additionally, though there may very well be former Truck Drivers Tom and Jerry who are now Gods themselves, they were irrelevant to our existence and we had no need to worship or even recognize them.

It didn't go over well. She soon left the church, vowing to never again worship Truck Driver Bob. I *finally* get where she's coming from.

With some people, though, I will NEVER get where they're coming from. A friend of mine was asked by her sister-in-law to make dinner for her wedding. The sister-in-law wanted to serve Chicken Marsala, and my friend, an excellent home cook, was happy to oblige. She worked with a tight budget, decided how much food she'd need, and bought everything for the dinner two days before the wedding. That very night her sister-in-law phoned, in tears: her mother had been horrified that the reception's dinner – served in an LDS church! – would contain Marsala wine, whether it cooked out or not. "After all," her mom told her, "the Bishop will be attending! So will your brother, and he was an Alcoholics Anonymous attendee for years!" (I'm assuming she feared that the taste of Marsala in his meal would tip him off the wagon and send him right back to AA.)

My friend very graciously re-planned the meal, returned the now-unnecessary ingredients and re-purchased everything she needed to cook for 80 people, and the dinner went off without a hitch.

Since that story is Word of Wisdom-related, allow me to divert to some WoW stuff: Brigham Young wanted funds from the general membership to support the Perpetual Emigration Fund, so he told everyone to give up their coffee and tea and alcohol and tobacco and use the money they would have spent on them for the sake of new converts. The WoW itself came about during a time when tea and coffee were expensive imports, *and* when prohibition was particularly popular. It also came about when vegetarianism was all the rage, and when Joseph's wife Emma complained particularly loudly about cleaning up chewing tobacco after meetings of the School of the Prophets. (Yes, there was a School of the Prophets.)

Joseph Smith never followed it, and Brigham Young commandeered a whiskey factory in Salt Lake City (which proceeds he desired) by sending the owner on a mission. (Historically accurate. Read up. Brigham's whiskey *sucked.*)

These days, coffee drinking will make you unworthy of a temple recommend, and alcohol – even after age 21 – is a tremendous sin, although it was CHRIST'S FIRST MIRACLE. (Not only was Christ's first miracle turning water into wine, it was the *best* wine. Christ was one heck of a vintner!) The Bible (very inconveniently) tells us that the juice of the fruit of the vine was intended to gladden the hearts of men. The LDS faith tells us that the juice of the fruit of the vine is wicked juice.

A few years ago an LDS friend of mine was diagnosed with fibromyalgia. She, too, is a Californian, and after much doctor-led experimentation with FDA-approved drugs (with horrendous side-effects), an LDS doctor(!!!) suggested she try medical marijuana. Being LDS, she had never in her life used marijuana, and told her doctor as much, intimating that marijuana was considered evil by her church and she could not use it. He then pointed out that he, too, was LDS, and he was also *her doctor*, and she should give it a go.

I wish I could tell her story the way she does. It literally moves me to tears. After a decade of suffering, she took her doctor's advice, and when she woke the next morning, she was, for the first time in over a decade, *completely pain-free*. No migraines, no full-body pain, *nothing*. After some months she "came out" on facebook, asking others she knew – particularly local members – to support her in changing her city's laws to make dispensaries safe and legal. She lost 36 friends overnight, all because she did what her doctor told her to do and then tried to persuade friends to support the one medication that gave her relief.

I confess, I was ignorant of the benefits of medical marijuana myself, not having had need, and having been raised in a church where "drugs" were considered evil. It had never occurred to me, prior to my friendship with this amazing woman, that there was any *legitimate* use for marijuana, nor had it occurred to me that everything God created was truly for a reason. Marijuana can be utilized or abused, as can any other drug currently on the market. For her it was a miracle.

So between Christ's miracle – *wine* – and my friend's miracle – *marijuana* – I began to *allow myself* to consider the benefits of WoW-forbidden things and read a book my fibro-ridden friend recommended, by Michael Pollan, called The Botany of Desire. The book traces the history of various plants based on man's love for and attachment to those plants, and both marijuana and apples are covered. Apples are not forbidden by the WoW, of course, but…I digress.

I realized something my friend had told me prior to my reading the book: We have Johnny Appleseed to blame for the Mormon church. I confess, my friend said it better, and so with her permission (and permission to edit her words), please consider the following:

"Okay, here it is: Johnny Appleseed is (indirectly) responsible for the Mormon church. You asked how. I'll explain, but first, read Botany of Desire by Michael Pollan. (He also wrote The Omnivore's Dilemma and In Defense of Food, in case you need some good reads!) No time? There's a documentary on Netflix. No time for that? Back to my dissertation, then.

"A couple hundred years ago a man named John Chapman - aka Johnny Appleseed - decided to Do the Work of the Lord. He was from a rather odd Christian sect: everything was to be done "the Lord's Way", which means all-natural. So what did he do? He went about the US of A spreading apple seeds EVERYWHERE.

"Problem is…well, look at it this way. You want a Braeburn, or a Honeycrisp, or maybe a Fuji apple. (I don't know why you'd want a Fuji, but…eh.) In fact, I want a Pink Lady…so I plant a bunch of seeds from my Pink Lady organic apple, and what do I get (many years down the line)? Trees with 95% inedible-y bitter apples; no Pink Ladies. So how do I get Pink Ladies? I graft in a portion of the Mother Tree, as it were, into a seedling, thereby "turning" the tree into a Pink Lady-producer.

"But Johnny didn't. Johnny spread seed willy-nilly, and a bunch of apple trees popped up all over the nation…95% of them bearing (you guessed it) inedible apples. What the heck do you do with inedible apples? You turn them into the only thing bitter apples are good for: HARD

CIDER.

"And what happens when apples (HARD CIDER) are plentiful, but water is practically poison? EVERYONE (we're talking kids, elderly, EVERYONE!) drinks hard cider. All the time, 'round the clock. And what do you get when everyone's drinking hard cider all the time? Rampant alcoholism, rampant spousal and child abuse, liver, kidney, brain, and developmental issues, and therefore.........

"A whole lot of pissed off born-agains up for prohibition and revivals!!! People everywhere meeting together to discuss the Demon Cider, to push for total abstinence from booze, and holy-rolling in the aisles at pop-up churches.

"Now, I ask you: Who was sitting in the aisles at those pop-up churches? The Smith family. And who got confused about all these churches and all their different ways of doing things (who, by the way, were actually all united, not by their belief in God, but by their hatred of hard cider!)? Why, little Joe Smith, Jr., of course. So what does he do? Prays in a grove. Who does he see? God the Father and His Son. What does he do then? Organizes the LDS church. How do we know he and his folks were prohibitionists? That fabulous story we all love to tell about when he was 7 and wouldn't drink booze to negate the pain of leg surgery. Had I been his dad, I've have forced the bottle between his teeth. But why didn't he? Prohibition, based on the appearance and misuse of hard cider, which cider came from bitter apples planted by Johnny, who did no grafting.

"Therefore: Johnny Appleseed is responsible for the formation of the Mormon church. Joe is responsible for the organization, of course (feel free to argue this was all part of the Lord's plan, and He organized it, but I'm not touching the spiritual implications at just this moment), but Johnny is responsible for the seeds, the trees, and inadvertently the cider and the crazies that followed...which led, of course, to Smith's search for truth."

Fascinating stuff, and from the perspective of an active Mormon, (even though you can tell her cognitive dissonance kicks in right there at the end,) truly amazing. Johnny Appleseed is responsible for setting the stage from whence sprang the LDS faith, and having properly run the gamut with that faith, I can honestly say I'm fairly certain God had *nothing* to do with it.

Strange, isn't it, how the WoW – a health code – could be one of the final nails in my LDS coffin, particularly since I generally still abide by it?

I have another coffin nail for you…a couple, actually.

Remember my old friend Joe, the guy who defended me on his mission and who eventually introduced me to my husband? He was a very dear friend with some pretty intense baggage, all stemming from an unstable priesthood holder who bestowed on him his patriarchal blessing back when Joe was about 16. You see, members of the church are entitled to one "major" blessing: a patriarchal blessing.

Tangent: Joseph Smith, Sr. was a patriarch…and he, along with all the other patriarchs, used to charge for blessings. You could get one whenever you wanted, as many times as you wanted…for $1.00, payable to the patriarch.

Each stake has a patriarch, whose job it is to be God's mouthpiece for the members of his stake once they have passed their worthiness interview to receive their blessing. He places his hands on your head, pronounces a blessing upon you (meanwhile recording it so he can later transcribe it for you; a copy of the transcription is then sent to Salt Lake to be attached to your membership record), and you spend the rest of your life studying that blessing and striving to bring to fruition all the psychic-like promises made, contingent, of course, on your worthiness.

Most patriarchal blessings are under two pages long; anything over is almost a badge of honor in the church, though very few people share or discuss their blessings with one another, charged to "keep them sacred."

Joe REALLY struggled. We were chatting alone one night when he divulged the source of his continual self-loathing: his patriarchal blessing was *15 pages long* and promised him that if he remained worthy, he would *CURE CANCER*…but if he failed, God would prevent him from discovering cancer's cure, and the entire human race would suffer until the Second Coming, Joe being their *only* chance. Mind you, Joe had very little interest in math or science and had already been introduced to (and become interested in) pornography. He thought he had failed before he'd even had the chance to try. He could not remove from his mind some of the images he had seen, try as he might, and could not make sense of some of his college-level math courses, sincerely believing his ability to learn had been blocked by the images of naked women in his head.

He hated himself. By the time he was back from a mission, his self-loathing had transformed into a sort of "whatever" attitude, and he was content to view porn, beat off, and study humanities, *knowing he had already failed a world full of people, past, present, and future.* As much as I adored him, he was a hard man to connect with, having utterly shut down his emotions in order to manage his self-hatred.

Another dear friend was tortured later in life by her patriarchal blessing. She had left the church a decade before, married in the Catholic Church (her husband was Catholic; she was ambivalent), and upon her very first pregnancy, she and her husband discovered their daughter was afflicted with a form of dwarfism. Right about the time they accepted the situation and made arrangements to accommodate a little girl who would be extra-little – about 34 weeks along in her pregnancy – they learned that the form of dwarfism their daughter had was fatal. She would not survive outside the womb, if she even survived birth, which was unlikely.

The tailspin this created for my friend and her husband is unthinkable by any standard, but my friend experienced, on top of that, something far worse. She had been promised in her patriarchal blessing (at 15 years of age, literally half a lifetime before) that if she remained righteous and married in the LDS faith, she would bear beautiful, healthy children and live happily ever after, but that if she chose a different path, God would be "unable" to bless her thusly.

Imagine, if you will, my friend on the delivery table of an abortion clinic for women whose pregnancies *must* be terminated – their daughter passed away in utero at 36 weeks – believing in her heart of hearts that *God had killed her firstborn child* because she had proved unrighteous and had not married a Mormon. I kid you not, I have to wipe the tears from my eyes even as I type this, more again as I edit and proof.

Had my friend not suffered enough, losing their daughter, their firstborn baby, to a crazy genetic malfunction? Did she really need to be tortured by the suggestion that that child's fate was what it was because she had fallen in love with a Catholic, or because she had decided the LDS Church was not for her? I *grieve* for her, my only consolation being that they now have a healthy, happy, adorable baby boy, bless their shattered hearts.

Utah is not just the porn capital of the US; it is also the anti-depressant capital. (I think I mentioned that already.) When you read things like the aforementioned items, it's not difficult to understand why. A painfully large percentage of LDS women take anti-depressants, for whatever reason, but I submit that in Utah, it is in part a direct result of their membership in the church, and because of the LDS counselors to whom they are sent for counseling. Take my friend Lisa, for example; her name is not Lisa, but that is hardly relevant to her situation.

Lisa was born and raised in the church and has recently left, now an atheist. Lisa is also bi-polar 1, her manic and depressive swings pretty severe. (I believe her dad is bi-polar, so in her case, it's genetic.) When she first decided she should see a counselor about her "mood swings," she talked to her parents, who sent her to her bishop; he, in turn, found her an LDS counselor and scheduled a session for her.

I say "session" because she only went once. After the first 15 minutes of her session, her counselor announced that she was indeed bi-polar, and she needed to go on medication right away. She asked if he would take her through to the end of her five sessions to better-determine whether or not she needed medication. He replied, "That's not how we do things. Drugs first, and treatment – *if it's even required* – after."

Lisa did not return to that counselor, and ultimately found a psychiatrist who specialized in bi-polar disorder who actually *counseled* her, put her on lithium after having seen her for a few months, then stuck with her for months more until they struck the right balance of medication and she had been able to work through many of her struggles.

The psychiatrist, incidentally, was *not* LDS.

And since we're on the subject of gross depression, I have to tell you more about my dear, dear friend Melissa. You see, we reconnected after many years, and I learned a great deal about her in a very short time, most of those things tremendously shocking.

First and foremost, Melissa served a mission abroad, and came home after nine months in the field. She was assigned to serve in a third world country, and her living conditions were atrocious. For nearly all nine months she was forced to live on the only available and affordable food: rice and fruit. She dropped 30 pounds and became so ill she could not work, and so depressed she could hardly function. Everywhere she looked were people living in poverty, their most basic needs – food, clothing, and shelter – not met. There she was, in turn, preaching a better life after death, offering "salvation" (*after* they committed 10% of their gross income to the church) when they lacked the basic necessities of life. She could not preach the love of God to these people she was not allowed to actually, physically help when God's love was nowhere to be seen, so the mission president sent her home.

For a year Melissa sat alone in her room, hardly eating, hardly speaking, hardly associating with anyone, losing herself in movies day after day and week after week. Drugs did not help, counseling did not help, and Melissa's mother, desperate to do anything for her despondent daughter, sent Melissa to a practitioner of Asian medicine. After three visits, acupuncture, and herbs, Melissa was given a clean bill of health and sanity. She put on weight again (though she is still quite trim), began to smile again, and eventually returned to her former self...minus any attachment to Mormonism. All she had seen of the LDS faith on her mission was a numbers game that took advantage of an entire people without offering them any respite or relief from their earthly woes. She was done.

She began dating again, and a couple years later she fell in love...with a woman. It was nothing she had ever planned or expected, but there was no denying her feelings: she was completely, utterly in love with a fantastic, gorgeous girl.

Last month Melissa went to visit her parents and finally "confessed" to her mom that she had fallen for a girl. Her mother was devastated and informed her that her girlfriend would never again be welcome in their home (now that she knows what they are to each other), and she just could not come to grips with the idea that her daughter was in a same-sex relationship. No matter how much she loved – and always would love – Melissa, this was just too big a sin for her to wrap her mind around.

The clincher? When her mother told her that it would be better that *she had never been born*. Now, that's motherly love!

Melissa, on the other hand, has proposed to her girlfriend, and the last time I spoke with her (particularly in light of her conversation with her mom), she told me she has never felt more free. May she *always* feel so.

I'm almost done – heaven knows I've said a lot! – but there are still a few more things I HAVE to say. Thankfully, they're not quite as dramatic as some of what you've already read.

Have you ever been to a Homemaking meeting? Of course you haven't. It's not called Homemaking anymore, anyway; it's now Home, Family, and Person Enrichment, which title is so long that most members of the Relief Society just call it "enrichment." It's *amazing*, the things you can learn from enrichment.

For example, back in the '70's, when my folks joined the church, Mom went to a homemaking meeting with pad and pen all excited and ready to learn about Herbs and Spices, the topic for the evening. When she arrived, she found a chair front-and-center and flipped to a blank page on her pad, eager to take notes, but did not spot any herbs or spices. There was a salt and pepper shaker on the counter, sure, but she was here to learn about *herbs and spices*. Up went the teacher to the front of the room, and she grabbed hold of that salt shaker and that pepper shaker (not even a mill) and placed them on the table in front, formally introducing her class to the evening's herbs and spices: salt and pepper.

Mom slammed her notebook shut and hunkered down for one of the most boring lectures she ever sat through, wondering vaguely how her fellow attendees could possibly be oohing and aahing. (Hey, when the Mormon food of choice involves cream-of-something casseroles, green jello, and "frog eye" salad – food to feed an army on the cheap – salt and pepper are a revelation!)

A couple months later she attended another homemaking meeting. The craft of the night was flyswatters. *Sequined* flyswatters. The women spent an hour and a half sewing sequins onto flyswatters "to beautify their homes." Ever since that night, Mom uses the term "sequined flyswatters" whenever she wants to describe (in two words) something she finds atrociously useless and stupid. (I love my Mom.)

I recently had my own grumbly homemaking experience, but nothing like that. Our current RS President believes everything we do should be spiritually uplifting, so she assigned her "cabinet" to put together a dinner for the women. I was looking forward to not having to cook, and to having my kids hang out in the priesthood-led nursery so I could socialize for 90 minutes like a grown-up. Even though I do not believe in the LDS faith, we have not yet left off attending, so I play my part, and I showed up.

The program lasted over two hours – the program, not the dinner! – and the food was just as bad as I've come to expect from any Mormon gathering, but it was the program that really threw me. We were supposed to walk away, I believe, feeling uplifted and strengthened. Instead I felt preached at, depressed, and deceived.

You see, I know the lives and situations of the women who presented their portions of the program (read: long-winded, self-aggrandizing or self-deprecating lectures), and they all have considerable struggles, yet there they stood, offering messages of hope, love, patience...the same hope, love, and patience very few of them actually possess.

Frankly, I went home and cried. For myself, for the presenters, and for all the women in attendance. I have no intention of ever going back to Enrichment...*ever*. I'm not sure why I ever went in the first place. This ward has been awful, and our last ward was awful, too, primarily because no one ever showed up.

Many odd things came out of that last ward, actually. It was by far the most political ward I've ever lived in. How so? When the bishop was released, there were two different men (other than the man called) who believed that *they* should have been called to be bishop. Neither was, so they both created their own factions in the ward, collecting people who were disappointed with the new bishop into one of three groups: supporters of the new bishop, supporters of Brother Stuffy, and supporters of Brother Obnoxious.

Knowing what a bishop has to deal with, I cannot possibly imagine anyone in their right mind would *want* to be a bishop, but that didn't matter to these to brethren. They seemed to feel they were passed up for a promotion, while the actual bishop would have given just about anything to turn down his "opportunity for progression."

The two opposing factions made Bishop's life a living hell as often as they could, and Brother and Sister Stuffy and pulled him into the stake president's office on at least two occasions to complain about how Bishop ran things in the ward. Meanwhile, Brother Obnoxious sat in the hall during gospel doctrine, openly watched sports games on his ipod with headphones in during priesthood meeting, and leaned back in his pew during sacrament meeting to catch a nap, amused when he discovered he had been snoring.

Anything to make Bishop miserable.

Brother Stuffy, by the way, was called as the ward gospel doctrine teacher and served for two months in that capacity until he preached one Sunday that during the plains-crossing, the women pioneers whose husbands were away on missions (or part of the Mormon Battalion) were "entitled" to use the priesthood – *as women* – to give blessings to their children, oxen, what-have-you. While I would love for that to be the case, it definitely was *not*, and once the leadership got wind of his teaching, he was immediately released.

It was not the only time in that ward that the membership preached what sounded like crazy doctrines...though in this next case, it actually IS LDS doctrine...just poorly-presented. One brother taught a gospel essentials class – a class made up of new and potential converts – and announced to the group that God's love is actually *conditional*; unconditional love was a misconception. Brother Conditional stated that God only loves those of His children who adhere to His commandments, meaning those who defy Him (via sin) cannot be counted among His people. In order to win back His love we must be baptized into the LDS faith and do our best to live perfectly, hoping in our heart of hearts that God sees fit to love us again.

I struggled to follow his line of thinking, wondering about the "God so loved the world..." scripture...or about the "nothing can separate us from the love of God..." scripture...or about...(You get the idea.) Needless to say, there were a whole lot of confused new and potential converts making missionary appointments later that week. One more thing: Brother Conditional was *still* gospel essentials teacher when we moved. After all, his crazy doctrines? They are REAL doctrines of the church!

Being a Mormon means that all the expectations laid upon you are either tedious (write in your journal every day, but make sure it's generally uplifting for posterity's sake!) or complicated (eat this, not that, wear this, not that, attend the temple this often, read this, not that, be sure you've got your year's supply...). To conclude this section with something not at all sensational, I refer to Jesus Christ, whose job it was to *simplify* the Mosaic law, not complicate it, add to it, or build on it. Matthew 11:30 is very clear: Christ's yoke is easy, and His burden light. Why, then, have I had so much to say about the church and all its history, rules, and expectations? Why have I (and others!) experienced so many awful things, so much heartache, and had so many red flags? If Christ came to simplify things, why does the Mormon Church add so damn much?

It's not the general membership doing that. It's the leaders. Why do it? It's about power, control, and the bottom line that pays for their six-figure incomes and Salt Lake shopping malls and "generous" donations for occasional disaster relief. It's about them, not us.

I can no longer support it. I can no longer sacrifice our hard-earned dollars to increase the church's bottom line. I can no longer raise my hand to sustain my leaders.

Simply put, I'm no longer a Mormon.

176

Now What?

Last year I visited an old friend, a born-again with a pastor-husband. She asked me to explain the Plan of Salvation for her as simply as possible, so I whipped out a sheet of paper and a pen and diagrammed away. When all was said and done she looked pensive, and when I asked her to tell me exactly what she was thinking, offensive or not, she said "Now I know why everyone says the Mormons are cultists. They worship a false Christ."

My dear friend, I have *loads* more reasons why Mormons are cultist, and almost none of them have to do with Jesus.

Having read all you have thus far in this book, please pause for a minute to consider my position. *If I walk away from this church, everything I have ever known evaporates instantly.* I forsake my faith (and therefore, my understanding of the way the universe operates). I will be (mostly) ostracized by my entire social network (and as a stay-home mom, that's major!) or publicly lambasted by them for the sins confessed herein. I will lose the support of most of my and my husband's family members. I endanger the sanity of my children, and I (could have) potentially face(d) divorce.

No, really. In fact, when I very first broke down and told my husband how I felt about the church, we debated divorce. For a couple of weeks. We hardly spoke during that time. He couldn't imagine that I was abandoning our eternal family, and I couldn't bear to speak until I knew whether or not he'd want to stay with me, faithless apostate that I'd become. (All's well now, by the way; he sat me down, assured me that he loved me more than life itself and could not bear the idea of being separated from me, and that he'd stay with me, come what may. Just like many of the rest of you married women, I have the world's GREATEST husband, and I will be eternally thankful to him for his love and understanding.)

I hear members of the Christian faith earnestly state that they would follow Christ no matter what, even if it meant leaving everything and everyone dear to them. I believe them, but some part of me thinks, "How convenient, to be able to promise something so dramatic, so *cavalierly*." I also know, as do they, that it is preposterously unlikely that any such thing would *ever* be asked of them.

Then there's *me*. What do I get if I leave? The rug pulled out from under me. *Live a lie, or live with the consequences.* And I'm *not* abandoning all and following after Truth. I'm not leaving everything for something better. I'm just leaving. Worse, thanks to the Mormon faith, I don't know *what* to make of Christ these days. (I'll get to that.)

You see, when you're born Mormon, you're immediately handed a pre-determined life course – a blueprint – that goes something like this:

1. Baby blessing
2. Primary attendance
3. Baptism at age 8
4. YW at 12, or Priesthood ordination if you're male
5. 4 years of Seminary, starting at age 14
6. BYU (no determined length of time for women; if we marry, we put our husbands through school)
7. Mission (for men, can come before or after college, but preferably at age 18)
8. Temple Endowment
9. Marriage in the temple (usually endowment and marriage are within a couple weeks of each other if you're female)
10. Your own babies blessed in the church (so the cycle continues)
11. Enforcing gospel education/expectations with your own kids
12. Endure to the end (a popular Mormon expression)

Should you defy that blueprint, family, friends, and social network evaporate. Worse, if you reach adulthood having followed that blueprint and you're on #12, all that's left for you to do is to "endure" (I'm astounded by the irony of their having selected that word) and you're set. But it also means that the church is so incredibly ingrained in your psyche – as you have no doubt seen it in mine as you've read this book – that walking away is nearly impossible.

Independent thought is nearly impossible, having lived this life. You see, in the church we rely on authoritarian figures to construct "our" opinions for us, and then we defend "our" opinions as best we can because they came from priesthood holders with a direct pipeline to God. I cannot count the number of times I have defended the church's stance on gay marriage, even when I felt utterly *unable* to do so. I mean, actually *psychologically unable*. I had no defense once or twice, and walked away feeling like I had let the church down because I couldn't adequately defend the opinion they'd given me. I had just never placed what I was feeling then in the context in which I now "get" it.

I was handed the opinion that wearing a cross was a symbol of Christ's agonizing death, and that we should refrain, "choosing" to focus instead on His resurrection. It just so happened that I've always liked decorative crosses – particularly the Celtic variety – so I spent the entirety of my youth feeling guilty for thinking a decorative cross was "pretty." I've stopped that now, and I wear a cross when I feel like wearing a cross, especially the Celtic one my husband bought me on a business trip.

I was handed the opinion that garments would keep me safe, and that showing my shoulders would both disappoint God and tempt men into illicit behaviors. It turns out that I'm incredibly comfortable with the body God gave me, and while I could not care less about showing it off, I have figured out which styles are to my best advantage where keeping my husband happy and/or dealing with normal and inclement weather and/or feeling good about myself are concerned. The few times I went out in public without garments (date night!) I felt horrendously guilty, which, of course, killed the mood when we got home from our date. I've gotten over all that now, and am determined to wear exactly what I feel best in at any given moment. My Mormon peers have accused me of wanting to follow immodest trends. Instead, I want to show the world that I see no need for garments, period.

It's not just about what I wear, though. Point is, opinions are often handed to us, rather than something we develop. This was abundantly clear recently, when my husband was on his way home from work.

In the church, we are promised the spiritual benefit of donating tithing is tremendous, but on this particular day my husband stopped for gas and encountered two young men pleading with the gas station customers for help. They had run out of both gas and cash and still had a 90-minute drive home. My husband wasn't sure whether or not to trust them – this is the modern world, after all – but decided that filling up their tank was no major sacrifice, and would prove a boon to them, honest or not. He ran his card through the pump, filled them up, then proceeded to fill up his own car. It just so happened that they were traveling the same way he was, and he said he followed them all the way. They had been honest about where they were headed, and had been incredibly grateful for his help.

When he got home, he told me about it, and we talked about whether filling up the kids' gas tank or paying tithing provided the greater spiritual benefit to my husband. Though we had always been taught the "right" answer, *after deliberating for ourselves*, we concluded the greater spiritual benefit of that $40 was derived by sharing with our fellow humans, not by sharing with the Mormon Church.

My husband's family would argue the opposite, but I am particularly blessed: my folks come from a different background. I'm blessed twofold, actually. My parents are converts who joined the LDS Church at about my age now, and they have been (mildly concerned, but still) utterly supportive of my coming to the realization that I do not believe.

I have been more honest with the general membership, too (who do not yet know that I'm leaving the church), in both attitude and appearance, and my husband has decided to be more honest, as well. A few weeks ago someone approached him at church and said, "Hi, Brother Samuelson! How are you?"

"Shitty," he replied. "Thanks for asking."

I love that man.

But where does that leave me, generally? I've already been all the way through the grief model, first with denial, (This "anti-Mormon" stuff can't be true!) and then anger, (for nearly four decades they lied to me?!) then bargaining, (Dear God, just tell me to stick with the Mormon Church!) then all-consuming depression, and finally acceptance: the LDS faith is bunk. I would argue I still sometimes experience anger and depression, (maybe even denial and bargaining,) but I believe there is one step beyond acceptance, and I've had a taste of it a few times.

It's ZEN.

Not just acceptance, but contentment.

When I put the church aside and am just "me", I'm content.

I'm Zen.

And it's wonderful.

I watched a documentary recently about a substance called DMT. Each of us – and every living thing – has it, and the human brain can produce it in quantity as required. Some refer to it as the "spirit molecule," and I can see their viewpoint: a large release of DMT in the brain can produce what are effectively visions.

One night, alone and desperate to know the truth about my childhood faith, I begged my Heavenly Father to tell me once and for all whether or not the Book of Mormon was "true." For one reason or another – either from sheer desperation, which prompted my body to produce DMT, or as a result of God stepping in personally and Himself prompting my body to produce DMT – I had a vision. Rather than answer my query, God expressed something so simple, yet so profound, I am about 70% certain that He exists (in some form or another). He "told" me that He loved me. I felt it in a way I had never imagined possible. *It was exquisite.*

There was quite a bit more to the experience, but it's far too personal to share. (No, not "sacred"; just *personal.*) That said, if my brain released DMT to convince me everything was okay and it was a simple biological response to an emotionally stricken woman's anxiety, but it turns out that God doesn't really exist (and that's our body's defense mechanism against emotional anguish or physical death), *I'm okay with that.* I'll die with a feeling of profound comfort and disappear, never knowing more. If, however, it *was* God, and I sincerely believe (and very much hope) that it was, *WOW.* God loves me. For no good reason at all, but simply because I exist.

And it's awesome.

Still I face grand difficulties ahead. *Never in my life* have I *ever* been expected to relate to different people. In elementary, junior high, and high school, I sought people similar to me to make friends. At BYU, I was surrounded by people similar to me. During the few (read: only) years of my career I lived in Utah, and most everyone was similar to me. As a married Mormon mommy, I am surrounded by other married Mormon mommies who are, you guessed it, similar to me. Okay, I'm a bit different from your average Mormon mom, but before now, the only thing that "mattered" was that I shared a belief system with my friends. Now I have no belief system, which leaves me wondering how to connect.

How on earth do I relate to people who are different?

Not very well.

I have never shown up to a party thrown by non-members that didn't freak me out to some degree. I couldn't relate, so I do what we Mormons are trained to do: I find the host and ask, "What can I help with?" The problem, of course, is that most non-member hostesses have it all so well-planned that there generally isn't much I *can* do, and when there is, I end up as a cook, server, or entertainer, so I'm *still* not learning to relate to "real" people.

Worse, I have fallen in to assuming that the general Mormon "nice to meet you" questions are okay. We met a couple who moved in a few doors down, newlyweds about our age, and the first thing I asked (after finding out they were newlyweds) was if and when they were planning to have kids. A) TOTALLY NOT MY BUSINESS, and therefore completely inappropriate. B) TOTALLY NOT MY BUSINESS, and therefore completely inappropriate!!! (I could add a letter "c" that said the same thing, but I'm guessing you get the idea.) But I come from a "ward family", and in a ward family, such questions are not only acceptable, they are expected. (Hence the reason I'm always prepared with the "I could die" answer.) Thanks to the church, I SUCK at socializing.

There are lots of things I suck at, coming out of Mormonism. I don't know how to drink booze. I went to a bachelorette party for an old friend where no one was LDS, and almost no one had a spouse or kids, even at our age. (See? Built in judgment and confusion at others' choices!) I had no way to relate to the women around me, so I settled down with a martini and finished the entire thing in under two minutes. My friend turned to me and said "Where did your martini go?" I told her I'd finished it. She and her friends laughed, and rightly so; it took them each a good 20 minutes to have one drink – *10 times as long as it took me* – and about a thousand times longer for them to be tipsy, while I was already floundering. Why? I'd never been taught to drink, and never learned to "enjoy" alcohol. I just figured if I didn't drink it quickly, the taste would make me retch and I'd never get it down, so down it went, and *boy*, did I feel it.

More disturbing, I don't know how to distinguish between "feeling the spirit" and feeling emotions. My emotions are flubbed; I have genetically-based chemical depression and take a low dose of corrective medication, but there are good days and bad days, and I never know exactly what I'm going to get. Does that mean that my bad days are a spiritual warning, or that my good days are the Spirit confirming the Truth of the Gospel? Of course not. It's just my crazy emotions getting the best of me. But then, what *is* "feeling the spirit"? How can I possibly recognize it? Is it different than what I was taught? How on earth can I learn to distinguish between feelings and spirituality?

How do I raise my children? My values are more-or-less the same, but now what? *What* do I teach them? And how do I get over the panic that they might not follow the blueprint? How do I cope with their not serving missions, attending seminary, going to BYU, or marrying in the temple? What will I do if they don't pursue eternal families...or any family? My panic is not justified, but it's inbred, and I still don't know what to do with that.

And where does all of this leave me with Jesus? I have been reading voraciously since I abandoned belief in the church, hoping to broaden my horizons and understand the world around me in a different light, in some other way than through the fog of the Urim and Thummim. I have read that Jesus was just a man with vision, or that Jesus never actually existed, and that the idea of Jesus was based on loads of other god-figures throughout history. Which is it?

When my mother was contemplating joining the Mormon Church, the missionaries stopped by one day to see how she was doing. She was reading the Bible and explained that, coming from the Catholic Church, where the scriptures were interpreted for her by the priests, she didn't know if she was "doing it right"; if she was reading the scriptures the "right" way. I confess I am currently in that same boat...and floundering

When I turn to most Christians to explain their beliefs and why I, too, should believe, I generally find their testimonies wanting. Many Christians praise Jesus, join a 45-minute sing-along on Sundays clad in shorts, t-shirts, and flip-flops, and then head home fulfilled, never really knowing what exactly they believe.

THIS IS INSUFFICIENT FOR SOMEONE LIKE ME!

How am I, over-educated in my faith as I am, ever going to be able to have an intelligent discussion with a Christian about whether or not Jesus and God are the same person when the person telling me that Jesus is actually God *has never studied the scriptures*? If I can prove to an unlearned Christian using the Bible that Jesus and God are two separate beings, how will they ever convince me that I'm wrong unless they are equally well-read? Or does that mean the evidence is insufficient, and they're wrong?

Most Mormons don't leave the church because they've been offended or because they're disenchanted with tithing, modesty, abstaining from alcohol, what-have-you, contrary to popular (Mormon) belief. They leave the church because they are intelligent, well-read people who discovered the key to the church's skeleton closet. In other words, they're bright, honest people who can no longer countenance the lies they've both lived and promulgated. They are people who, once they realize atrocities like polygamy, polyandry, slavery, and blood atonement lurk just below the surface of our faith, can no longer pretend that such ideas are obsolete, nor continue in assuming that Jesus Christ would back or advocate such obscene doctrines. When they leave, they are left with very few religious options, and they – *WE* – are searching, but most of what we encounter is ambivalence and ignorance in the various faiths we explore. I don't know how to read or interpret the Bible, except through Mormon spectacles. Heck, these days I'm not even sure the Bible *is* "God's word"!

(The flood? Magic hair? A pillar of salt and angel-rapists? Really?!)

Those of us who leave need help, guidance, support, and love. We're starting over, you see. I've just been launched into a world where I have to form *my own* opinions, where my family is *not* "forever", where my marriage is *not* "eternal", and, therefore, where *nothing* is certain.

NOTHING. And where does *that* leave me? Moving forward one step at a time, hurt but hopeful, and desperately seeking Truth, no matter how difficult that truth may be for me to cope with or accept.

Please help me. Please help us. While you cannot exactly understand our position unless you, too, have experienced it, I pray fervently that this book has helped in some small way for you to relate to those of us who are searching for answers, for understanding, and for love.

We are alone.

If the human race is to have any hope of evolution, we need each other, and we need you. Because if I'm no longer a Mormon…*what am I?*

I guess I'll find out eventually.

With all my heart,

Regina

[i] The study was conducted by Express Scripts Inc., a St. Louis-based pharmacy benefits management company, which tracked prescriptions of 24 drug types in about 2 million people selected at random from its 48 million members. Those studied were enrolled in privately managed health-care programs, and the information gleaned from the study is intended for use by HMOs. Medicare and Medicaid recipients were not included in the study. Quoted in the LA Times, 2-20-2002.

[ii] The study used data from anonymous credit card sales from a top-10 Internet porn provider that operates hundreds of Web sites offering a wide variety of adult entertainment, then correlated that data with ZIP code information. Quoted in the Salt Lake Tribune, 3-2-2009.

[iii] Of Young's 55 wives, 21 had never been married before; 16 were widows; six were divorced; six had living husbands; and the marital status of six others are unknown. At the time of Young's death, 19 of his wives had predeceased him, he was divorced from ten, and 23 survived him. The status of four was unknown. Quoted from Jeffrey Odgen Johnson, "Determining and Defining 'Wife' — The Brigham Young Households", _Dialogue: A Journal of Mormon Thought_, vol. 20, no. 3 (Fall 1987), pp. 57–70.

[iv] "This Greeley is one of their popular characters in the East, and one that supports the stealing of Niggers..." Journal of Discourses, 5:119.

If you get a chance…

1. Baker, Lee B. Mormonism: a Life Under False Pretenses
2. Brodie, Fawn. No Man Knows My History: the Life of Joseph Smith
3. Burningham, Kay. An American Fraud: One Lawyer's Case Against Mormonism
4. Romney, Park. The Apostasy of a High Priest – The Sociology of an American Cult
5. Stenhouse, Fanny. Tell it All: the Story of a Life's Experience in Mormonism
6. Webb-Young, Ann-Eliza. Wife No. 19
   (For more reader-recommendations and former-LDS book reviews, please visit at www.nolongeramormon.blogspot.com!)

About the Author

Regina Samuelson is a now-apostate member of the Mormon Church, thanks to years of inner turmoil, serious reflection, and earnest questioning and study. A California girl, she was raised LDS, educated at Brigham Young University (the foremost educational institution owned by the LDS Church), and was married at an early age in the temple, with children following shortly thereafter. She has held a number of callings during her tenure in the faith, from nursery worker to Young Women's President, and as a Relief Society, Gospel Essentials, and Gospel Doctrine teacher. Her last calling (as Gospel Doctrine teacher) prompted her to thoroughly examine her faith and its many inconsistencies, modern, historical, and scriptural.

Even now she and her family are deliberating over her next step - pretending everything is just fine, or walking away entirely - and her book I'm (No Longer) a Mormon represents the struggle she faces.

Hungry for more?

Follow Regina's continuing journey (and leave comments for her!) on the web by visiting **www.nolongeramormon.blogspot.com**.

To discuss the possibility of a personal appearance (if and when Regina is revealed) at book clubs, church groups, etc, please direct all inquiries to inlamregina@gmail.com.

Made in the USA
San Bernardino, CA
12 August 2013